Arising Incense

A Believer's Priesthood

JEANNE METCALF

1st Printing 2017
Copyright © 2017

2nd Printing:
Cëgullah Publishing
Copyright © 2022

3rd Printing 2025
Cegullah Publishing & Apologetics Academy
www.cegullahpublishing.ca

All rights reserved.

ISBN # Textbook: 978-1-926489-57-5
ISBN # Workbook: 978-1-926489-58-2

Cover photo © i-Stock # 47555973
Cover design by Jeanne Metcalf.

COPYRIGHT MATTERS

This book is an original manuscript by the author, protected by international copyright laws of Canada. Therefore, this author's work *may not be reproduced*, in part or in whole, or stored in a retrieval system, or transmitted in any form or by any means, electronic, mechanical, photocopied, recorded or otherwise for commercial use without the *prior written* permission of the author. However, it is possible to receive permission to use short quotations for personal use, or use in a group study, or for permission to copy certain passages, or to make portions of the writings available for overhead viewing. Simply, contact the publisher[1] to request it.

SCRIPTURE MATTERS

All scripture quotes originate from KJV[2], public domain. However, the name of God appears as YeHoVaH, not LORD. See appendix for more information.

---

[1] Contact us at www.cegullahpublishing.ca.
[2] KJV refers to all humankind as "man". Unless the passage itself refers to a particular male person, apply the message to all humankind, regardless of gender.

DEDICATION

This book is dedicated first, to the Great High Priest, Yeshua, Whose eternal priesthood functions after the order of Melchizedek. Secondly, to every believer in Yeshua who truly longs to please YeHoVaH in every aspect of their being, and so learn to function within the order of their God-ordained priesthood. [3]

---

[3] On the crown the Hebrew says, "holiness unto YeHoVaH".

COURSE 205
ARISING INCENSE

CHAPTER	DESCRIPTION	PAGE

SECTION 1: PRIESTHOOD:
From Adam to Aaron

	Introduction	9
1.	Adam's Priesthood	17
2.	Noah's Priesthood	33
3.	Abraham's Priesthood	47

SECTION 2: PRIESTHOOD:
From Aaron to the Cross

4.	A Kingdom of Priests	63
5.	A Chosen Lineage	79
6.	Aaronic Priesthood Tabernacle	
	Part 1	95
	Part 2	105
7.	Incense & Intercession	117

COURSE 301
ARISING INCENSE (continued)

SECTION 3: PRIESTHOOD:
From the Cross, forward

8.	A Change of Priesthood	135
9.	A Change of Tabernacle	
	Part 1	149
	Part 2	161

10.	A Far Greater High Priest............	169
11.	A Far Greater Priesthood	
	Part 1............................	185
	Part 2............................	203
12.	Incense & Intercession............	217

APPENDIX

About this Author................................	257
About CP & AA.......................................	258
About King James Version........................	242
A Name to Honour................................	234
Contact Information..............................	258
Order of Melchizedek – Messianic View......	233
Other Books by this Author.....................	250
Salvation's Message..............................	244
Salvation's Prayer & Lifetime Commitment.	248
Scripture Index.....................................	253

COURSE 205

SECTION 1:

PRIESTHOOD

From Adam to Aaron

Introduction

As I looked up from my filing job, where I stood behind an opened filing cabinet, I saw a male figure. He walked through the front door of the office and headed my way. He was over six feet tall, had thick jet-back hair, a warm and pleasant smile. Coming closer towards me, he reached out his hand to shake mine. Returning the gesture, with a big smile, I stretched out my hand to shake his, stepping forward at the same time.

Suddenly, without thinking, I opened my mouth wide and shrieked. In stepping forward to greet the young man, so enraptured by him, I forgot to close the bottom file cabinet drawer. Tripping over it, I began to tumble to the ground.

Gravity was about to have its own way as I speed towards an unwelcomed encounter with the floor. Quickly, the young man lunged forward interrupting my fall, catching me with his strong waiting arms.

Humiliated but grateful for his help, I brushed aside my embarrassment and managed to ask him if I could help him. He told me that he was the new branch representative for the finance company where I worked. This introduction to the company, neither one of us forgot!

Time went on in that little company office, however, the young man stayed only a few months. When he left, our relationship continued and one year later, the two of us stood before a church altar. Holding hands in a marriage ceremony, we made a lifetime commitment to each other.

It has been nearly half a century since the day of our unique introduction. Looking back, I chuckle to myself on how I literally fell for my husband! Also, I giggle at the Heavenly Master's plan, and this promised husband for whom I prayed.

Indeed, he entered my life in a way, my wildest imagination, could never dream up. This remarkable, unexpected, surprising answer to my prayers and the life to follow, all began with one of God's unique, divine appointments!

A BIBLICAL DIVINE APPOINTMENT

As I think of such Divine appointments, ones that change your life forever, I think of a day when a worshipper of false gods,[4] named Abram, met the creator of the universe. After Abram's initial encounter with YeHoVaH of glory,[5] his life changed, forever. Indeed, when God, Who initiated the Divine encounter, stepped into Abram's life, He totally shattered the mould for Abram, totally changing his destiny. Little did Abram know that those moments when God interrupted his life's journey, that he'd develop a strong and long-term covenant relationship with God Almighty, and that, through the relationship, God would bless all nations.

This relationship with God came at a high cost as Abram learned many lessons in his personal commitment to God. From the beginning,

---

[4] Joshua 24:2 "And Joshua said unto all the people, Thus saith YeHoVaH God of Israel, Your fathers dwelt on the other side of the flood in old time, [even] Terah, the father of Abraham, and the father of Nachor: and they served other gods."

[5] Acts 7:2 "And he said, Men, brethren, and fathers, hearken; The God of glory appeared unto our father Abraham, when he was in Mesopotamia, before he dwelt in Charran,"

following the initial encounter, God began to separate Abram from all he knew.

Genesis 12:1-3

> 1 ¶ Now YeHoVaH had said unto Abram, Get thee out of thy country, and from thy kindred, and from thy father's house, unto a land that I will shew thee: 2 And I will make of thee a great nation, and I will bless thee, and make thy name great; and thou shalt be a blessing: 3 And I will bless them that bless thee, and curse him that curseth thee: and in thee shall all families of the earth be blessed.

Commitment to continued fellowship with God meant leaving behind his father,[6] and all his kindred, meaning his siblings and their offspring, too, and travel to a land, about which he knew nothing.

Abram's relationship with God matured, whereby Abraham became a prophet and priest unto God and moved into a covenant-style

---

[6] While God commanded Abram to leave his father, Abram brought his father along with him, as well as his nephew, Lot. After his father, Terah, died, Abram's journey with YeHoVaH stepped up a notch, and after his nephew Lot eventually left to go his own way, this covenant relationship with God moved forward to its full potential. This covenant required Abram's full obedience!

relationship with God. Their relationship was so unique and blessed that, like a marriage, Abram's[7] named changed to reflect the unity in his relationship with God. God gave him a new name, Abraham, which in effect took the last "ה" (the "heh" or the breath of God) from God's name and added it to both Abram and Sarai's name. This new name showed the oneness of this *covenant agreement* between God and Abraham and Sarah.

PRIESTHOOD AND COVENANT

Abraham's priesthood with God and the covenant agreement between them is found in the book of Genesis, the book of beginnings. Therein are found records of the covenant and priesthood of Abraham, with its altar and sacrifice. Genesis also mentions and gives inference to other priests, some existing before, during and after Abraham. The believer's priesthood, today, is spoken within the context of the Apostolic scriptures.

A BELIEVER'S PRIESTHOOD

In this book, as we explore some of those priesthoods and covenants in the Bible, you'll see the various responsibilities, altars and sacrifices of priesthood found in the Hebraic

---

[7] Abram's wife, Sarai, also had the same letter incorporated into her name, changing it to Sarah.

scriptures. As we study the Aaronic priesthood, you'll recognize its heavy duties and enormous responsibilities. Then, in shifting our focus to the New Covenant and its priesthood, you'll see a powerful contrast and liberty. In the final chapters of this book, as we look at the New Covenant and the believer's priesthood, indeed, you should recognize the far greater priesthood of the believer, as well as identify the believer's altar and sacrifice.

AUTHOR'S PRAYER FOR YOU

Dear reader, the way I see it, a believer's priesthood is the entire embodiment of a life lived for Messiah. As you read and study this material, may there arise an awareness of your priesthood in that light. May such propel you to move forward to operate in your priesthood and find in it *true fulfilment*. This can only bless God, you and others, whose lives you touch for God. May YeHoVaH enable you, dear one, to grasp and embrace the road leading to the greatest depth of your relationship possible with Him, that of your priesthood.

AUTHOR'S REMINDER

Yeshua said in John 8:32
    32 And ye shall know the truth, and the truth shall make you free.

True liberty comes by hearing and receiving the truth. To receive truth, sometimes there is a battle. When that is the case, determine, ahead of time, to resist temptations to toss confronting truths aside. Determine now, with God's help, to shift your mindset into full gear to live the life God designed for you. Embrace that life, within the context of the New Covenant, *including the expression of your priesthood,* and let the hold of any former, erroneous teachings shatter.

Adam's Priesthood   1

"IN THE BEGINNING" are the words used to open the book of Genesis, and it is to this book we go to discover the first operative priesthood. We find that priesthood, initiated by YeHoVaH, in the life of Adam after the fall. At that time, when the Adamic priesthood came into being, we hear also of a unique covenant, whereby God made a promise to Adam. We'll look at that momentarily, but first, we need to go back, to the time before the fall, to look at a very important commission God gave to all human kind, beginning with Adam, a commission God expected Adam to obey!

Let's look at Adam from the context of God's creation.

Chapter 1: Adam's Priesthood

Genesis 1:26-28

26 ¶ And God said, Let us make man in our image, after our likeness: and let them have dominion over the fish of the sea, and over the fowl of the air, and over the cattle, and over all the earth, and over every creeping thing that creepeth upon the earth. 27 So God created man in his own image, in the image of God created he him; male and female created he them.

28[8] And God blessed them, and God said unto them, Be fruitful, and multiply, and replenish the earth, and subdue (3533) it: and have dominion <07287>[9] over the fish of the sea, and over the fowl of the air, and over every living thing that moveth upon the earth.

It has interested many a scholar to see the words, "subdue" and "dominion" in the above scripture. These words do not portray a quiet and tranquil garden in perfect unison with God and man. Yet, these words are there.

Let's look at them:

---

[8] Genesis 1:28 commissioned both Adam and Eve.
[9] We'll look at this word shortly.

Subdue	Strong's #3533
כבש	Pronounced kaw-bash'
This is a primitive root and a verb, which denotes action. That action is to keep under, if necessary by force. It means subjugation.	

To fully understand this word, we'll look at some other scriptures, which use this word:

2 Samuel 8: 11

> 11 Which also king David did dedicate unto YeHoVaH, with the silver and gold that he had dedicated of all nations which he subdued <03533>;

Here, King David took an offering given to him by Toi, the King of Hamath, as a blessing for David after he defeated an enemy. It is clear, from this and other scriptures, it was David's habit to do this, after he subjugated his enemies. That subjugation was physical, elevating David as King above his enemies.

1 Chronicles 22:18

> 18 Is not YeHoVaH your God with you? and hath he not given you rest on every side? for he hath given the inhabitants of the land into mine hand; and the land is subdued <03533> before YeHoVaH, and before his people.

In this scripture, King David gave orders to leaders in his kingdom to help David's son, Solomon, to build the temple. David clearly recalls God's hand with David as he subdued his enemies. Again, this is a physical subjugation, by which David ruled.

2 Chronicles 28:10
> 10 And now ye purpose to keep under <03533> the children of Judah and Jerusalem for bondmen and bondwomen unto you: but are there not with you, even with you, sins against YeHoVaH your God?

This instance shows the words of a prophet speaking against the ruler of a pagan nation. Earlier, due to the sins of His people, YeHoVaH allowed Israel to be defeated in battle. In this passage, the prophet reminds the enemy they also have sinned. He then challenges their purpose to put into bondage the men and women of Judah. These few references, along with the other 10 uses of this word, present the idea of bringing something into submission, subjection or bondage.

Returning, then, to the word used by God in His commission to Adam, why use the word "subjection"? The only answer lies in the fact that, indeed, something needed to be put under. But what? In discovering that fact, we need to look at one other scripture, which relates God's purpose for man in the Garden:

> Genesis 2:15
> And YeHoVaH God took the man, and put him into the garden of Eden to dress it and to keep <08104> it.

This word interpreted as *"to keep"*, in the original Hebrew language, is the word "שמר", pronounced "shar-mar". It carries with it the idea "to observe", "to beware", or "to guard". Seven times, in the KJV translation of the Bible, this word was interpreted as ***"watch"***.

Coupling this idea of *watching or keeping guard*, with the idea of subdue, we understand there was something in the garden, for which Adam must be on his guard. In hindsight, we know that something was "sin" waiting to enter the world and bring with it death.

Adam, warned by God, had a responsibility to guard or watch out for that which needed subjugation. Adam, according to scripture, had all he'd need to stand victorious in that encounter. We find that in the word ***"dominion"***, from the commission in Genesis 1:28.

Let's read it again:

Genesis 1:28
> 28 And God blessed them, and God said unto them, Be fruitful, and multiply, and replenish the earth, and subdue it: and have dominion <07287> over the fish of the sea, and over the fowl of the air, and over every living thing that moveth upon the earth.

Dominion	Strong's #7287
רדה	Pronounced raw-daw
It is a primitive root, a verb (denoting action). It means to rule, to prevail over, to reign, to rule as a king.	

Looking at this word, in its origin Hebrew picture language, we see this word clearly denotes authority, with the application of victory. In simple terms, Adam and Eve's commission came with the necessary authority, even the necessary ability, to stand and not fall, in this encounter with "sin".

Many Jewish Rabbis look at the commission and see this role of Adam, as that of a king. In addition, they believe that as God instructed Adam to "subdue" the earth, that action by Adam was deemed by God as service to Him, and hence, when fulfilled, became an act of worship. Many rabbis, from the information they see in the Hebrew text, conclude that Adam walked in a role of High Priest for the order of Melchizedek, even before the fall.

Unfortunately, not all Hebraic scholars agree. What many do agree upon, however, is that Adam's original commission set him up as a king. Thus, when Adam disobeyed God's command, at that same time, he failed to exercise his kingly role, within his commission to rule. Through that failure, Adam opened the door for both sin and death to enter the earth. As a direct result of Adam's disobedience, he, and his seed after him lost *access* to the authority that he once possessed.

After the fall, as God reached out to Adam, He promised a restoration and at that same time, initiated Adam's priesthood. We see that in the following verses where God made a blood covenant with Adam and Eve, initiating also, Adam's priesthood.

> Genesis 3:15
> 15 And I will put enmity <0342> between thee and the woman, and between thy seed and her seed; it shall bruise thy head, and thou shalt bruise his heel.

To see the covenant God made, we'll first look at the word "enmity":

enmity	Strong's #0342
איבה	Pronounced ay baw'
This is a noun, which KJV interprets as "enemy". Others interpret the word as division.	

Using Strong's meaning, we see that God promised to put an *"enemy"* between ha satan and the woman. That enemy would stand between the enemy's seed, which is sin, and the woman's seed, which is a reference to one to come, born of woman.

Looking at Genesis 3:15, with this meaning in mind regarding enmity, we, therefore, recognize *the first mention of the promised One* to come is an enemy of sin. Looking further into this word "enmity", by using the Hebrew picture language, we see something rather amazing.

Remember, the word enmity, shown on the previous page is, in Hebrew "איבה", (pronounced ay baw').

Letter	Name	Amongst its Meaning:
א	aleph	(ox) Strong, powerful leader
י	yod	(arm & hand) stretch forth, reach
Parent root:		*Powerful leader with arms stretched out*
ב	bet	(tent) person, home, nation, world
ה	heh	(man with arms stretched out) victory through God's breath
Child Root		*person, with arms stretched out attains Victory through God's breath*
Overall Meaning: *a powerful leader, with arms stretched out, whose deeds (work) touches people (nations) obtains victory by the breath of God.*		

(Later, you'll enter this information into your workbook.)

That promised one to come is a powerful leader, who stretches out His arms, on behalf of all people in all nations. His victory happens through the power of the breath of God, or the Holy Spirit. *What a picture of the crucified Saviour ... What a picture of the cross!*

In the Hebrew word picture of this word "enmity" we clearly see the promised one to come, is indeed the enemy of sin. He'd regain all Adam lost, and as an enemy of sin, gain a victory to benefit all humankind.

Here we not only see a promised one, but also a covenant, for shortly after this promised one, we see God's action shedding the blood of an animal. We'll look at that shortly. For now, let's read more about this covenant established with these fallen ones, from whom all humankind came.

> Genesis 3:16-21
> 16 ¶ Unto the woman he said, I will greatly multiply thy sorrow and thy conception; in sorrow thou shalt bring forth children; and thy desire shall be to thy husband, and he shall rule over thee. 17 ¶ And unto Adam he said, Because thou hast hearkened unto the voice of thy wife, and hast eaten of the tree, of which I commanded thee, saying, Thou shalt not eat of it: cursed is the ground for thy sake; in sorrow shalt thou eat of it all the days of thy life; 18 Thorns also and thistles shall it bring forth to thee; and thou shalt eat the herb of the field; 19 In the sweat of thy face shalt thou eat bread, till thou return unto the ground; for out of it wast thou taken: for dust thou art, and unto dust shalt thou return.

20 ¶ And Adam called his wife's name Eve; because she was the mother of all living. 21 ¶ Unto Adam also and to his wife did YeHoVaH God make coats of skins, and clothed them.

If you read the text, *carefully*, you'll see God *cursed the serpent* (verse 14)[10] *and the ground* (verses 17 & 18). Contrary to what many scholars teach, God **did not curse** the woman or the man. God did not curse that human life which He earlier blessed. His desire for them was salvation, and that, they received by faith.

We see that as they expressed their belief in His Promised Messiah!

In verse 20, we read that Adam gave his wife a new name, "Eve", meaning mother of all living. When Adam renamed his wife to "Eve", he understood and believed the promised one to come, not from the woman to whom he listened and then disobeyed God, thus bringing in sin, but through the "mother of living". This is evidence of Adam's faith and salvation.

---

[10] Genesis 3: 14 And YeHoVaH God said unto the serpent, Because thou hast done this, thou art cursed above all cattle, and above every beast of the field; upon thy belly shalt thou go, and dust shalt thou eat all the days of thy life:

Later, in Eve's life, we see her faith and salvation as she named her son:

Genesis 4:1
> 1 And Adam knew Eve his wife; and she conceived, and bare Cain, and said, I have gotten a man from YeHoVaH.

Cain's name, in the Hebrew picture language shows Eve's trust in God, and her belief that this child came from God. We see that also in the text in verse 1. While Eve misunderstood the fact that Cain was not the promised one, her declaration here shows she believed the promise of God.

Moving on to Verse 21, we see God making coats of skins for Adam and Eve for clothing. To clothe with skins meant that an animal, chosen by God, must die. Its blood, its life, must be released from it for this clothing to come about.

In the act of providing this covering for Adam and Eve, most biblical scholars believe God chose a lamb. It is further believed that here, with this act of clothing completed, Adam received his priesthood, learned about the altar, saw the sacrifice prepared and offered and received the message *that sin requires an atonement.*

Adam, having been isolated from his earlier kingly authority, embraced this mantle of animal skins, being clothed in it, after sin's atonement. From then on, he served YeHoVaH in this servant manner of priesthood[11]. From this point, onward, then, we see the beginning of the *priesthood of Adam*[12].

Adam's priesthood, he taught and passed on to his son, Abel. We see this priesthood operative in Abel's life. As Adam outlived Abel, we find the priesthood passed down, next, within Adam's line, to his godly son, namely Seth, bypassing Cain.

HIGHLIGHTS OF ADAM'S PRIESTHOOD

As we close this chapter on Adam's priesthood, we see some highlights of an Adamic priesthood. First, it is an honour, a privilege *to serve God* in such a capacity, and thus, as a service, it is worship unto God. Secondly, Adam's priesthood was initiated by God. It is believed this priesthood, with its altar and sin

---

[11] Some Jewish scholars do not believe Adam set aside his royal mantle, but they believe he kept it and passed it down generation to generation. This we will discuss later, when we discuss the priestly order of Melchizedek.

[12] Many theorize that these "coats" God made from skins *began the idea of the tallit* as a symbol of the priesthood, with Adam installed as a High priest.

offering, God showed to Adam when God made "coats" for the man and his wife[13]. If scholars are correct in this assumption, then God taught Adam what he knew regarding an offering for sin. However, scripture is not clear on this subject. This we presume happened when YeHoVaH made coats for Adam and Eve, and later see God accept an offering presented to Him by Abel, Adam's son.[14]

Thirdly, the priesthood is a God-ordained, merciful expression of a life lived for God. It is a personal and compassionate way of *bridging the gap between fallen man and a holy God*, Who requires sin's atonement to establish a relationship with Him.

As we look at *priesthood*, from its early beginnings in Genesis, we see its main operation is a mediation, where the priesthood positions its priest to stand in the gap for others. Priesthood, as God established it, finds God's appointed servants first saved, then reaching to seek the God of all heaven and earth for His forgiveness and help in the lives of others.

---

[13] Genesis 3:20

[14] Genesis 4:4 And Abel, he also brought of the firstlings of his flock and of the fat thereof. And YeHoVaH had respect unto Abel and to his offering:

From a scriptural viewpoint, from Genesis to Revelation, we see that, as long as there is sin upon the earth, *a priesthood must exist.* That priesthood may change its order or form, meaning it may look slightly different, as it shifts from one covenant to another; however, it will always mediate and petition for forgiveness, then, **turn and bless humankind on behalf of God.**

Priesthood is something humankind, living on this sinful earth, *will always need.*

A BELIEVER'S PRIESTHOOD

Every born-again believer is called to a priesthood. As we go about discovering and then highlighting that priesthood, you'll see that it has *similarities* to Adam's priesthood, as well as to another, called "Aaronic", which originated under the Law. Both priesthoods have an altar, a sacrifice and *mediate for forgiveness of sins.* However, the New Covenant believer's priesthood functions *far beyond* that of Adams, Noah's, or Abraham's. It also *far surpasses* the dynamics of the Aaronic priesthood established under the Law. While, at this point you might not understand, nor perhaps agree, please keep this one thought in mind:

 *A believer's priesthood is an integral part of their life. As such, it is important that we understand how it functions.*

Knowing the order to which we belong is, therefore, imperative.

Noah's Priesthood — 2

We meet Noah in Chapter 5 of Genesis. In between the record of the fall and Adam's priesthood seen in Chapter 3, Chapter 4 relates the generations of Adam. In these few verses, a span of time is covered as it lists Adam's descendant such as Cain and Abel. In the story of these two brothers, we learn of Abel's acceptable offering, and Cain's rejected offering. We are shown Cain's hatred for his brother as well as the murder in Cain's heart, to which he yielded and slew his brother.

Genesis 4 tells us happenings in the ungodly line of Cain, then brings forth new hope, proclaiming the birth of Seth, Adam, and Eve's last son, who bore the priesthood of Adam. We further hear of descendants from the godly line of Seth, with sons such as Enos, Cainan, Mahalaleel, Jared, and Enoch.

At Enoch, the lineage record temporarily stalls to give us some highlights of this godly man named Enoch. We hear that Enoch walked with God, and from the Apostolic scriptures written by Jude, we hear "Enoch, also, the seventh from Adam, prophesied of these (false prophets), saying, Behold, YeHoVaH cometh with ten thousands of his saints, to execute judgment upon all, and to convince all that are ungodly among them of all their ungodly deeds which they have ungodly committed, and of all their hard speeches which ungodly sinners have spoken against him.

These are murmurers, complainers, walking after their own lusts; and their mouth speaks great swelling words, having men's persons in admiration because of advantage[15]. Genesis, further, tells us that Enoch walked with God, and God translated Enoch into heaven[16].

Next, Genesis 4 moves on to speak of Enoch's son, Methuselah. In that very name, we hear the prophetic message of his father, Enoch speaking judgment to the wicked world at that time. We

---

[15] Jude 1:14-16

[16] Genesis 5:24 And Enoch walked with God: and he was not; for God took him.

see that in the meaning of "Methuselah". Taking a literal translation of it, it means "when he is dead it shall be sent". In the life of Methuselah, we see he lived the longest of any human being, 969 years. In the length of his life, we see God's hand of mercy, not willing that any should perish!

Methuselah had a son named Lemech, who in turn had a son named, Noah. Genesis takes time to speak about Noah, as well as the fulfilment of the promised judgment declared by Enoch. First, before going there, let's look at Lemech, at a time when he named his son, Noah. It is here we see by the name Noah, words which speak clearly of a future action of God:

Genesis 5:29

> 29 And he called his name Noah, saying, This same shall comfort us concerning our work and toil of our hands, because of the ground which YeHoVaH hath cursed.

Lemech's words gives clear evidence that Noah brings comfort to them regarding the work and toil of their hands, because it was hard working with the ground, as it was cursed by God. Many biblical authorities believe the word "comfort" would be better rendered as "rest". Authorities, who analyse this verse, believe "rest' is an applicable translation of "comfort", showing here Lemech's prophetic mantle, as he believed God, that through Noah's time, the righteous would have comfort or rest from the constant presence of evil around them. About that wickedness, the bible says:

Genesis 6:5-8

> 5 And GOD saw that the wickedness of man was great in the earth, and that every imagination of the thoughts of his heart was only evil continually. 6 ¶ And it repented YeHoVaH that he had made man on the earth, and it grieved him at his heart. 7 And YeHoVaH said, I will destroy man whom I have created from the face of the earth; both man, and beast, and the creeping thing, and the fowls of the air; for it repenteth me that I have made them. 8 ¶ But Noah found grace in the eyes of YeHoVaH.

Great wickedness is the topic of these verses, but before exploring this, we're going to take a side-step to understand something God, Himself, prophesied before the flood.

Up to Noah's day, the normal life span of humankind, before the flood, was anywhere from 779 to 960 years.[17]

---

[17] See chart on next page

LIFE SPAN FROM ADAM TO LEMECH[18]		
Name	Died at	Reference
Adam	930	Genesis 5:5
Seth	912	Genesis 5:8
Enos	905	Genesis 5:11
Cainan	910	Genesis 5:14
Mahalalel	895	Genesis 5:17
Jared	962	Genesis 5:18
Enoch	365+[19]	Genesis 5:23
Methuselah	969	Genesis 5:27
Lamech	777	Genesis 5:31
Average Lifespan = 908 years[20]		

It seems odd, considering this fact, that God said,

Genesis 6:3

> 3 And YeHoVaH said, My spirit shall not always strive with man, for that he also is

---

[18] This chart, in part, was sourced via Wikipedia.

[19] Enoch was raptured so his life continues on with YeHoVaH and thus, it does not say he died!

[20] Without including Enoch in the average.

flesh: yet his days shall be an hundred and twenty years.

Why would God say this before the flood? Some believe YeHoVaH declared the number of years to the flood, while others think He had another purpose. For those who believe that the flood would occur in 120 years, Genesis would need to be not in complete chronological order. Reason being, if one follows the chronological order given in Genesis, it is only 100 years from the time of this word until the flood.

For those who believe the latter theory, God decided that the life expectancy of humankind would be less, thus lessening man's opportunity to do great evil upon the earth, and of course, lessen the timeframe of the Holy Spirit striving with each individual person to repent. If the latter theory is true, it would not mean that people could not live past 120 years, after the flood because a few people did *(Abraham and Sarah being two such people.)*

After the flood, however, we do see humankind's life span lessening, shortened considerably, as time passed by, and so much so that King David declared a much lower life expectancy:

Psalm 90:10

> 10 The days of our years are threescore years and ten; and if by reason of strength they be fourscore years, yet is their strength labour and sorrow; for it is soon cut off, and we fly away.

In returning to the wickedness operative in the time of Noah, we see God pronounced judgment upon all flesh. He said,

Genesis 6:11-13

> "11 ¶ The earth also was corrupt before God, and the earth was filled with violence. 12 And God looked upon the earth, and, behold, it was corrupt; for all flesh had corrupted his way upon the earth. 13 ¶ And God said unto Noah, The end of all flesh is come before me; for the earth is filled with violence through them; and, behold, I will destroy them with the earth."

WHERE WAS THE PRIESTHOOD?

Since this book is about priesthood, we need to understand that the priesthood of Noah, which was operative[21], could not save the wicked world at that time. We find reference to that in a scripture in a much later book:

---

[21] It is seen operative after the flood.

Ezekiel 14:14

> 14 Though these three men, Noah, Daniel, and Job, were in it, they should deliver but their own souls by their righteousness, saith YeHoVaH GOD.

This reference is to Judah, at a time prior to when Nebuchadnezzar destroyed it. Noah, named amongst the intercessors, in his time, managed to save the souls of his family and no more!

NOAH'S PRIESTHOOD IN OPERATION

In Genesis 8, we see Noah's immediate response from exiting the Ark, which took him and his family through the flood:

Genesis 8:20-21

> 20 ¶ And Noah builded an altar unto YeHoVaH; and took of every clean beast, and of every clean fowl, and offered burnt offerings on the altar. 21 And YeHoVaH smelled a sweet savour; and YeHoVaH said in his heart, I will not again curse the ground any more for man's sake; for the imagination of man's heart is evil from his youth; neither will I again smite any more every thing living, as I have done.

NOAH'S SIN OFFERING TO THE LORD

First, Noah built an altar and chose the sacrifice. As he operated in his role as priest, God saw Noah's sacrifice to Him as a sweet savour, meaning it was very pleasant to YeHoVaH. Noah's priesthood, at this point in time, presented God with a sin offering. We know this for several reasons:

1. Noah makes a blood offering from a clean animal unto YeHoVaH. *(Unclean would never make an appropriate sin offering!)*
2. God declares this offering by Noah as a "sweet savour". "Sweet" in Hebrew implies *rest and peace,* while "savour" suggests sacrifice. Since God, Himself, called this offering a sweet savour, and like that of Abel's, had respect for it, it can be no other offering after the state of the world, than a sin offering.
3. On those same lines, with a sin offering in place, even though the imagination of man's heart is evil from his youth, God no longer needed to enact such a severe judgment for those who sinned against Him. Noah's priesthood put before YeHoVaH a very acceptable sacrifice, by which peace and rest came upon the earth.
4. Verse 21 presents God's word never to curse the ground any more, for the sake of humankind. The broken curse suggests also,

the offering was a sin offering. This verse, also references back to Lemech's comment about Noah when he said, "29 And he called his name Noah, saying, This same shall comfort us concerning our work and toil of our hands, because of the ground which YeHoVaH hath cursed."[22] Here we see Noah's life fulfilled the prophecy over his life by his father, Lemech.

As the text continues in Genesis, we see that God says that He will not curse the ground any more for man's sake, *for the imagination of man's heart is evil from his youth.* God promised, also, not to destroy every living thing by water ever again. Those promises came in the *form of a covenant between God and, the earth,*[23] *and every living creature of all flesh.* The sign of the covenant was the rainbow. This promise of this covenant YeHoVaH made to Noah **3 *times*:**

Genesis 9:8-17

> 8 ¶ And God spake unto Noah, and to his sons with him, saying, 9 And I, behold, *I establish my covenant* with you, and with your seed after you; 10 And with every living creature that is with you, of the fowl,

---

[22] Genesis 5:29

[23] Genesis 9:13

of the cattle, and of every beast of the earth with you; from all that go out of the ark, to every beast of the earth.

11 And *I will establish my covenant* with you; neither shall all flesh be cut off any more *by the waters of a flood*; neither shall there any more be a flood to destroy the earth. 12 ¶ And God said, This is the token of the covenant which I make between me and you and every living creature that is with you, for perpetual generations: 13 I do set my bow in the cloud, and it shall be for a token of a covenant between me and the earth. 14 And it shall come to pass, when I bring a cloud over the earth, that the bow shall be seen in the cloud:

15 *And I will remember my covenant*, which is between me and you and every living creature of all flesh; and the waters shall no more become a flood to destroy all flesh. *16 And the bow shall be in the cloud; and I will look upon it, that I may remember the everlasting covenant between God and every living creature of all flesh that is upon the earth.* 17 And God said unto Noah, This is the token of the covenant, which I have established between me and all flesh that is upon the earth.

Noah became a husbandman of the ground and planted a vineyard.[24] He then made some wine, which he drank. Noah became intoxicated, an action which confuses many people who read about this in Genesis. They wonder why such a Godly and righteous man became drunk.

To understand Noah's actions, we need to know one main important factor:

the fermentation processes of the earth changed.

After the flood, fermentation occurred much quicker than prior to the flood. Noah, unaware of the change, drank the fermented wine which consequently, made him drunk. As Noah lay drunk, one of his sons commit an act of sin against Noah. When Noah awoke, he knew what his son had done to him. Noah then pronounced a judgment upon his son:

> Genesis 9:24-27
>> 24 ¶ And Noah awoke from his wine, and knew what his younger son had done unto him. 25 And he said, Cursed be Canaan; a servant of servants shall he be unto his brethren. 26 And he said, Blessed be YeHoVaH God of Shem; and Canaan shall be his servant. 27 God shall enlarge

---

[24] Genesis 9:20

Japheth, and he shall dwell in the tents of Shem; and Canaan shall be his servant.

In the time of Noah, the priesthood included blessings, and as can be seen here, cursings. This curse Noah pronounced upon his son. No sin offering was offered for his son, either.

NOAH'S PRIESTHOOD PASSED ON

Noah, in expressing judgment upon his son, also blessed Shem. In doing so, we have the godly line shown to us, that is, the blessed line by which, it is believed, the priesthood followed, as expressed in the life of Shem. As we close the pages of Noah, we see the new earth take form, along with its many inhabitants.

Moving on, in Genesis, looking at humanity, we see many lived ungodly lives, while a few, lived godly lives. Genesis lists the genealogy, activities good and bad of humankind. We hear of Nimrod, and the beginning of the kingdom of Babel.[25] We hear of the earth dividing in the time of Peleg[26], along with the establishment of the aisles of the Gentiles, with their land divisions.[27]

---

[25] Genesis 10:9-10
[26] Genesis 10:25
[27] Genesis 10:5

Genesis 10:32

> 32 These [are] the families of the sons of Noah, after their generations, in their nations: and by these were the nations divided in the earth after the flood

Chapter 11 presents us with the tower of Babel and God's judgment to scatter the people, confounding their language, thus enforcing God's edict, as recorded below, to Noah and his family:

Genesis 9:1

> 1 ¶ And God blessed Noah and his sons, and said unto them, Be fruitful, and multiply, and replenish the earth.

With the earth divided, the people scattered. It soon became time for God, in His Divine Mercy, to call out Abram, who He would rename Abraham. It was through Abraham's line, that God's covenant promise of salvation for all humankind would come, that great salvation as promised to Adam and Eve.

Abraham's Priesthood   3

Abraham was man of faith, a man who experienced the sight of the glory of God. He was a man who physically talked with God as YeHoVaH visited him in his own tent[28]. Abraham taught the ways of YeHoVaH to his entire family as well as all his servants, ensuring none of them worshipped false gods. Scripture shows Abraham as a man who built various altars along certain places of his sojourning and shows him communing with God on a regular basis. We also see where God called Abraham a prophet.

Scripture outlines Abraham and his life before YeHoVaH, specifying his lineage, his promised inheritance, as well as a long and detailed list of

---

[28] Genesis chapter 18.

Abraham's descendants. Much information detailed about those descendants includes a particular tribe from which God sets aside priests unto Himself[29]. Scripture in Genesis speaks of Abraham's death, and burial, too.

This legacy of Abraham, as related to us, is very descriptive, leaving out very little about God's covenant partner. Through this man, Abraham would come a promised seed, through whom the whole earth would be blessed. Yet, there is no specific mention of Abraham as a priest.

ABRAHAM'S ALTAR

While no specific mention of Abraham as a priest can be found, we see that Abraham built an altar and made sacrifices. One such incidence is found in Genesis 12:

Genesis 12:7-8

> 7 And YeHoVaH appeared unto Abram, and said, Unto thy seed will I give this land: and there builded he an altar unto YeHoVaH, who appeared unto him. 8 And he removed from thence unto a mountain on the east of Bethel, and pitched his tent, having Bethel on the west, and Hai on the east: and there he builded an altar unto

---

[29] This priesthood was known as the Aaronic priesthood.

YeHoVaH, and called upon the name of YeHoVaH.

Abraham, by his actions, operated as priest and thus had a priesthood.

TYPE OF PRIESTHOOD

When trying to identify the order of priesthood to which Abraham belonged, some Messianic scholars see Abraham as operating not in a priesthood like that of Adam, but rather in the role of a king and priest like unto the order of Melchizedek. To fully comprehend how this conclusion is drawn, these believes look to another book, outside of the Bible, called "The book of Jasher", which apparently helps them to draw such conclusions. In looking at this order of Melchizedek, some believe that Melchizedek was Shem, the third son of Noah, who would then be a direct living ancestor of Abraham[30].

As scholars review the meeting that took place between Melchizedek and Abraham, they read that Melchizedek shared bread and wine with Abraham[31]. From that and other clues they find in the text, they conclude this as the place and time when Shem pass on his priestly and kingly

---

[30] See Appendix (Order of Melchizedek) for more information on this subject, as per Messianic viewpoints.

[31] In accordance with some Messianic teachings, it was here that blessing of Shabbat began following this meeting of Abraham with Melchizedek.

priesthood to Abraham. They see Abraham functioning, from that point on, in the priesthood of Melchizedek.

However, as we look at Abraham's life, staying within the scriptural text, we do not see this claim. We do, however, see the priestly office operative in Abraham's life, even though not specifically mentioned. So, to determine the type of priesthood by which Abraham operated, we should see some place in his life where Abraham clearly functioned as a king.

ABRAHAM, PRIEST & PROPHET

Through the covenant relationship that unfolded and developed between God and Abraham, we see the man matured to the point where God called Him a prophet. At one point, we see God instructed a pagan king, who innocently but wrongfully acted against Abraham, to have Abraham offer a prayer of healing.

Genesis 20:7

> Now therefore restore the man his wife; for he is a prophet, and he shall pray for thee, and thou shalt live: and if thou restore her not, know thou that thou shalt surely die, thou, and all that are thine.

In this one scripture, where we see Abraham called a prophet, we see *he operates as a priest,* seeing the king (and his household[32]) healed! From this and other scriptures, we see Abraham performing priestly activities. Although wealthy and head of a tribe, he was not declared a king, out rightly.

Instead of a priesthood well defined in the office of a king and priest, we see this humble man's priesthood concealed in his whole manner of living. This is as it should be, for as commented much earlier in this book, a priesthood should be the entire embodiment of a life lived out for God!

With these thoughts in mind, if we must put a label on the type of priesthood lived out by Abraham, the only order of priesthood operative within the godly line was that which followed from Adam. Abraham, then, most likely operated in the Adamic order of priesthood.

FATHER OF NATIONS

Earlier we saw how Abraham's intercession healed a king and his household. Scripture also shows us that through God's covenant keeping abilities with Abraham, YeHoVaH orchestrated

---

[32] Scriptures to support this are found in the homework for this section.

Abraham's life so that he fathered a great nation, and through him every nation upon the earth was blessed[33]. This aspect of Abraham's life, the Apostle Paul spoke of in his message to the Galatians:

Galatians 3:8

> "8 And the scripture, foreseeing that God would justify the heathen through faith, preached before the gospel unto Abraham, saying, In thee shall all nations be blessed."

Here we see that Abraham had the gospel spoken to him! What a relationship he had with God! How all things should fade in the light of Yeshua, including the lifestyle of Abraham's priesthood!

SIDESTEP: WHEN THE BIBLE IS SILENT

In looking at Abraham's life, looking for clues to the priesthood whereby he functioned, we do not find specific data to give clear evidence. When the Bible is silent, and that silence peeks our curiousity, how are we to respond? Do we stay within the clear parameters of scriptures, or dare we step outside to discover a truth?

---

[33] While blessing is a function of every father (and mother), it is also a function of a priest.

To answer that question, let's approach the subject from another angle. When Divine Inspiration excludes a fact, what does that absence mean? Regarding Abraham's priesthood, we might ask the question, "What priesthood shone the brightest, in the time of Abraham?" That priesthood, of course, is none other than the priesthood of Melchizedek.

Genesis 14:18-20

> 18 And Melchizedek king of Salem brought forth bread and wine: and he was the priest of the most high God. 19 And he blessed him, and said, Blessed be Abram of the most high God, possessor of heaven and earth: 20 And blessed be the most high God, which hath delivered thine enemies into thy hand. And he gave him tithes of all.

Let's examine that encounter with Melchizedek, look at Abraham's behaviour with Melchizedek and then see God's message.

ABRAHAM MEETS MELCHIZEDEK

Abraham was the victor of an intense and furious battle, in which he went to war with some kings in the land simply to rescue his nephew, Lot, from captivity. In those days, captivity usually meant slavery and torment.

After Abraham wins the battle, he returns to his place of lodgings. Somewhere, as

Abraham brings back the people and their goods to freedom, the King of Sodom goes out to meet Abraham, still at this point called Abram. Along with this king, rides another King, Melchizedek, also a priest. His name, when divided shows the following:

- "Melek" in Hebrew means king
- "Tzedek" meaning righteousness

By interpretation, this man's name means, King of Righteousness. He lived in Salem, meaning "place of peace". Most Jewish scholars believe this place to be Jerusalem, long before King David took it from the Jebusites to make it the capital city of Israel.

Melchizedek brings forth water and wine, which suggests some kind of a covenant ceremony. Then, he blesses Abram, who pays tithes to the king. This action of paying tithes, as well as Abram being the recipient of the blessing, shows Melchizedek to be the greater of the two. Apostolic scriptures verify that:

Hebrews 7: 5-7

> "5 And verily they that are of the sons of Levi, who receive the office of the priesthood, have a commandment to take tithes of the people according to the law, that is, of their brethren, though they come out of the loins of Abraham: 6 But he whose descent is not counted from them

received tithes of Abraham, and blessed him that had the promises. 7 And without all contradiction *the less is blessed of the better.*"[34]

In looking at this priesthood of Melchizedek, we see that he was indeed a priest and a king, however, *scripture omits something else regarding this King.* It does not show his earthly lineage.

This is a significant factor because Genesis, *the book of beginnings*, as we have already outlined, is about *lineage*. If Divine Inspiration deemed it *important* to name the lineage of Melchizedek, it would have entered it. Again, Divine Inspiration left this out, also. Why? The message from this missing information we receive from the book of Hebrews:

Hebrews 7:1-3

> 1 For this Melchisedec[35], king of Salem, priest of the most high God, who met Abraham returning from the slaughter of the kings, and blessed him; 2 To whom also Abraham gave a tenth part of all; first being by interpretation King of righteousness, and after that also King of Salem, which is, King of peace; 3 Without father, without mother, without descent, having neither

---

[34] Bold and italic, the author's.

[35] Melchizedek is spelt this way in the Apostolic writings.

beginning of days, nor end of life; but made like unto the Son of God; abideth a priest continually.

From the book of Hebrews, in the Apostolic writings, we see how that, which "Divine Inspiration" excluded, made a way for those in the early church, who wrote our Apostolic scriptures, to point a finger straight to Yeshua: To this target all Hebraic scripture, first, points! Yeshua and His mission were hidden within the types and shadows of those Hebraic scriptures.

ABRAHAM'S HUMBLE LIFE

In closing this chapter on Abraham, and this first section of priesthood operating before the Law was given, we see from Adam to the time when God brought Abraham's descendants out from bondage, a priesthood entailed an altar and a sacrifice.

In Abraham's life we see a detailed description of such a priest of God who was set apart for God. He learned to possess great faith, faced the challenges in his life leaning upon God and looking for God's solutions. That example Abraham gave and while his priesthood might not seem as glorious to us as that of Melchizedek, it is certain his life before God shone bright and gave a pleasing fragrance!

 # SECTION CONCLUSION

We have looked at the Adamic order of priests whereby an altar and sacrifices make up the operation of a priesthood. While not specifically mentioned, *other than in the life of Abraham,* it is worth mentioning that God's choice of priest, within this Adamic order, was from the *godly line*. That tells us the lifestyle of the priest was as important to God as the offering of sacrifices.

In looking at priesthood, we also saw that Genesis, with its missing information, and the book of Hebrews interpretation of that absent data, make it very clear that the message we need to hear, thus far, regarding priesthood, is first, that faith in God and righteous service go hand in hand.

Next, we see an order of priesthood God marks as extremely note-worthy. Not because of glamour or glitter, but rather as an early pointer to priesthood, with reference to the Messiah. We see that message as recorded in the Psalms.

Psalm 110:4

> 4 The LORD hath sworn, and will not repent, Thou art a priest for ever after the order of Melchizedek.

In the book of Hebrews, we clearly see the long-awaited Messiah, Yeshua, is the one of whom Psalm 110 speaks:

Hebrews 7:14-19

> "14 For it is evident that our Lord sprang out of Juda; of which tribe Moses spake nothing concerning priesthood. 15 And it is yet far more evident: for that after the similitude of Melchisedec there ariseth another priest, 16 Who is made, not after the law of a carnal commandment, but after the power of an endless life. 17 For he testifieth, Thou art a priest for ever after the order of Melchisedec. 18 For there is verily a disannulling of the commandment going before for the weakness and unprofitableness thereof. 19 For the law made nothing perfect, but the bringing in of a better hope did; by the which we draw nigh unto God.

Yeshua, as a High Priest after the order of Melchizedek, shows *the far surpassing excellence of this priesthood* above any other priesthood, including the Aaronic priesthood, established in the time of Moses, which we'll study in the next section. In the meantime, please keep in mind the greatness and superiority of the order of this priesthood, known as that of Melchizedek. Its greatness is a key factor when trying to understand and embrace the New Covenant believer's priesthood.

PRIESTHOOD WITHOUT A TABERNACLE

In looking at every priesthood in the Bible, from Adam until the inauguration of the Mosaic Tabernacle, we see the main aspects of priesthood were very simple: a priest's sanctified life, their faith in God, their altar and their sacrifice. Those operating in the godly line of priests within the book of Genesis, used their priesthood to express their worship to God and bless Him. From that service, they then blessed humankind.

In all the operation of priesthood duties within the book of Genesis, we are not told of any godly priesthood operative within the setting of a tabernacle or temple erected to God. Operating *without a tabernacle*, the priesthood in Genesis has something in common to the New Covenant!

However, believers today offer spiritual sacrifices in a spiritual tabernacle, and of course belong to a greater priesthood!

1 Peter 2:5

> 5 Ye also, as lively stones, are built up a spiritual house, an holy priesthood, to offer up spiritual sacrifices, acceptable to God by Jesus Messiah.

THE TERM ADAMIC PRIESTHOOD

Each of the three men of God, studied in this first section, are patriarchs of the faith. The term "Patriarchal Priesthood" is what Bible students often called this priesthood. While that title does fit, today, there is a use of that term which has given it new meaning. Patriarchal priesthood, now, refers to a certain religious cult who sees this as their type of priesthood. To avoid confusion, we'll use the term Adamic. This is the common term used by many Jewish people to classify the priesthood prior to the law. For the purposes of this book, we'll call their priesthood "The Adamic Priesthood".

COURSE 205 cont'd

SECTION 2:

PRIESTHOOD

From Aaron to the Cross

A Kingdom of Priests 4

In the opening chapters of the book of Exodus, we find God's call to bring out of bondage, those children of Israel who went down into Egypt to escape a famine in their land. With a mighty hand God brought them forth. Exodus 15 nicely recaps some of the highlights of that deliverance[36]:

Exodus 15:11-19

> 11 Who is like unto thee, O YeHoVaH, among the gods? who is like thee, glorious in holiness, fearful in praises, doing wonders? 12 Thou stretchedst out thy right hand, the earth swallowed them. 13

---

[36] If you are not familiar with the story of the children of Israel exiting from Egypt, please read about it in your Bible.

Thou in thy mercy hast led forth the people which thou hast redeemed: ***thou hast guided them in thy strength unto thy holy habitation.*** 14 The people shall hear, and be afraid: sorrow shall take hold on the inhabitants of Palestina. 15 Then the dukes of Edom shall be amazed; the mighty men of Moab, trembling shall take hold upon them; all the inhabitants of Canaan shall melt away. 16 Fear and dread shall fall upon them; by the greatness of thine arm they shall be as still as a stone; till thy people pass over, O YeHoVaH, till the people pass over, which thou hast purchased.

17 Thou shalt bring them in, and plant them in the mountain of thine inheritance, in the place, O YeHoVaH, which thou hast made for thee to dwell in, in the Sanctuary, O YeHoVaH, which thy hands have established.[37] 18 YeHoVaH shall reign for ever and ever. 19 For the horse of Pharaoh went in with his chariots and with his horsemen into the sea, and YeHoVaH brought again the waters of the sea upon them; but the children of Israel went on dry land in the midst of the sea.

---

[37] Bold and Italics the author's addition.

God, indeed, is the strength of Israel, as can be seen in His leading of them to leave behind Egypt for a place of promise. Verse 13 and 17, which have been bolded and highlighted, relays some specifics regarding their destination:

Exodus 15:13

> 13 Thou in thy mercy hast led forth the people which thou hast redeemed: thou hast guided them in thy strength unto thy holy habitation.

Exodus 15:17

> 17 Thou shalt bring them in, and plant them in the mountain of thine inheritance, in the place, O YeHoVaH, which thou hast made for thee to dwell in, in the Sanctuary, O YeHoVaH, which thy hands have established.

From these two verses, we know God's plan is to bring His children into the place where He lives, in other words His holy habitation. Secondly, He wishes to plant them in the mountain of their inheritance, in the place made for God to dwell. That place is God's sanctuary, the one He built with His own hands.

These scriptures show God's desire to bring His children unto Himself and live in their midst. Unfortunately, the people that came out of Egypt were not ready to experience the exact plan, as God's perfect will demanded. Instead, they rebel against God and His plans for them. In mercy, God gives them a secondary plan. Let's pick up the story from where the children of Israel surround the earthly mountain of God.

Exodus 19:1-6

> 1 ¶ In the third month, when the children of Israel were gone forth out of the land of Egypt, the same day came they into the wilderness of Sinai. 2 For they were departed from Rephidim, and were come to the desert of Sinai, and had pitched in the wilderness; and there Israel camped before the mount.
>
> 3 And Moses went up unto God, and YeHoVaH called unto him out of the mountain, saying, Thus shalt thou say to the house of Jacob, and tell the children of Israel; 4 Ye have seen what I did unto the Egyptians, and how I bare you on eagles' wings, and brought you unto myself. 5 Now therefore, if ye will obey my voice indeed, and keep my covenant, then ye shall be a peculiar treasure unto me above all people: for all the earth is mine: 6 And ye shall be unto me a kingdom of priests, and an holy nation. These are the words which thou shalt speak unto the children of Israel.

Verses 1 to 2 tell us of the arrival of the children of Israel upon the mountain of YeHoVaH. God calls Moses up to the top of the mountain and gives him a message to relay to the children of Israel. God's message to Israel conveys 4 major points:

1.	*Remember:*	<ul><li>I am He that brought you out of Egypt</li><li>I carried you on eagles' wings and brought you to Me</li></ul>
2.	*Obey:*	<ul><li>My voice</li></ul>
3.	*Keep:*	<ul><li>My covenant</li></ul>
4.	*Be:*	<ul><li>A peculiar treasure to me, above all people</li><li>a kingdom of priests</li><li>a holy nation</li></ul>

These 4 major points outline the requirements of those who wish to exist as God's people:
- Part 1: **REMEMBER.** Summarizing the wording here, it is to remember the One who brought you to Himself, Who bore you out on eagle's wings. Don't look to another.
- Part 2: **OBEY.** The word translated as obey comes from the Hebrew word, שמע, pronounced shaw-mah'.[38] It

---

[38] Strong's Concordance # 8085

means to hear and follow through by doing what was heard.
- Part 3: **KEEP**[39]. The word translated as "keep" comes from the Hebrew word, שמר, pronounced shaw-mar'. It means to watch over, to guard, to take care to protect. This means living within the parameters or guidelines given in the covenant, taking great care to see the behaviour matches what's required.
- Part 4: **BE**. Summarizing the result of keeping the first three parts occur, God's own become:
  - a peculiar treasure to God, above all other people
  - a kingdom of priests
  - a holy nation

These 4 points summarize nicely what God desired for His people and how their lives would take shape, if they did their part. After hearing the conditions, the children of Israel gave their answer:

Exodus 19:8
8 And all the people answered together, and said, All that YeHoVaH hath spoken

---

[39] Strong's # 8104

we will do. And Moses returned the words of the people unto YeHoVaH.

With their agreement in place, YeHoVaH planned to come and speak with the people. Certain conditions needed to be put into place to ensure the people survived the experience. Boundaries were set up to ensure the people kept a proper distance. Moses ensured the people were sanctified, and they washed their clothes, a sign they must be clean before YeHoVaH. Then on the 3rd day, God descended upon Mt. Sinai.

Smoke ascended like a smoking furnace and the mountain began to quake. Trumpets began to sound louder and louder and louder! Then YeHoVaH came upon the mount and called Moses up to the top, and Moses went. God sent Moses back down to ensure the people would not break through, and in doing so, die. In YeHoVaH's warning, He also included warnings for the priests … wait a minute … what priests?

Before the giving of the law and the establishment of the Aaronic priesthood, every family had a priest in their household, namely the Father. Also, the first-born son played an important role, as he took on the role of High Priest of the family. These priests as well as their duties, followed the Adamic Priesthood, as did Adam, Noah and Abraham.

Returning to the mountain scene, God had not yet given the Aaronic priesthood, however, He invited the priests to sanctify themselves, and later He warned, they not break through the designated boundaries and touch the mountain. That action would cause them their life. Moses, therefore, in obedience to YeHoVaH, went down to the people and gave them the words of God.

Exodus 20 relays what Moses spoke to the children of Israel: *the 10 commandments of God.*

Those gathered around the mountain, hearing thunderings and seeing lightnings, backed away from the mountain. Standing at a distance, they told Moses, "You go speak with God. We will hear from you, but not from God, in case we die!" Moses drew near to the thick cloud of darkness. Later, he conveyed to the people some further behavioural conditions to serve YeHoVaH.

Finally, after Moses relays the message from God, he writes it all into a book.[40] Next morning, he rises early and builds an altar at the mountain base, in accordance with the

---

[40] Exodus 24:4

instructions God gave him for such an altar.[41] Young men come and offer burnt offerings and peace offerings to YeHoVaH.

Moses takes one half of the blood from the offering and puts it in basins. With the first half, he sprinkles the altar. Next, Moses reads the book of the covenant[42] to the audience of people gathered before him. They all respond with their commitment,

> **"Whatever God says, we will do it".**

With the positive response from the people, Moses sprinkles sacrificial blood on the people and says,

> Exodus 24:8 b
>
> "Behold the blood of the covenant, which YeHoVaH hath made with you concerning all these words."

Next, with sacrificial blood sprinkled, Moses takes Aaron, his brother, Nadab and Abihu, (Aaron's sons) and seventy elders of Israel. They saw the God of Israel and ate and drank with Him[43].

---

[41] Exodus 20:24-26
[42] Exodus 24:7
[43] Exodus 24:10-11

Moses, in accordance with God's invitation, goes up higher on the mountain, leaving the camp in charge with the elders, Aaron and Hur.

On the mountain top, Moses receives the tablets of stone from YeHoVaH, which contain the 10 commandments. Moses also receives instructions to build the Tabernacle and its instruments, after the pattern that God showed to Moses on the mountain[44]. As Moses tarried forty days and forty nights, the people thought Moses was not returning to them.

Concerned that they've lost their leader, who was their contact with God, they decide to make a god for themselves out of gold. This god they can touch, they can control, and they can worship, their own way. Aaron makes them the calf, and calf worship takes place on the foot of the mountain of God.

Up to this point in the book of Exodus, the priesthood still followed that of Adam, Noah and Abraham, but with this action, *they moved away from the Adamic Priesthood and its service to the One True God. As they moved into idolatry, they defiled the sacred priesthood entrusted to them.*

---

[44] Exodus 25:9

Aaron, one privileged to meet with God and eat and drink with Him, remembers not the warnings of God. He makes an altar for the golden calf and proclaims a feast to it, on the pretence it is for YeHoVaH. Rising early in the morning, they offer sacrifices to the golden calf, and eat and drink, together. These very actions are those of making a blood covenant, almost identical to what they did with Moses and YeHoVaH forty days earlier.

MOSES RETURNS

Moses, under God's instructions, came down from the mountain with the tables of stone. He breaks those stone tablets, sees the golden calf broken up, puts the dust in the people's drinking water and makes them drink it. Moses then cries out, "Who is on YeHoVaH's side? Let him come unto me!" Gathered to Moses came the sons of Levi. Following a word of judgment, the Levites gird their swords, and slay 3,000 people that day. Moses then returns up the mountain to make atonement for their sins.

GOD SHOWS MERCY

Moses speaks with God, making intercession for the people. God extends His mercy to the children of Israel and YeHoVaH gives Moses another set of the 10 commandments written on stone. Moses comes again to the people, relays the necessary requirements for YeHoVaH's

Tabernacle, and the people of Israel set out to make it. When finished, they set it up, in accordance with YeHoVaH's command, on the first day of the first month. After the necessary ceremonies were complete, the glory of God fills the tabernacle.[45]

A CHANGE OF PRIESTHOOD

It is interesting to note two important things:

- In Exodus 28, God tells Moses to make Aaron and his sons priests unto Him, thus changing the priesthood from Adamic to Aaronic.

- Aaron, even though he participated in the golden calf offence before God, was forgiven. His priesthood would be inaugurated shortly after the tabernacle was erected. His sons were consecrated into the priesthood as well.

In all this, however, there came a shift in priesthood. The Patriarchal priesthood ceased. Now, one tribe would be chosen from amongst the twelve to become God's order of priesthood. This shift is important! Why?

Earlier, God set out His goals for His people. We looked at it earlier in this lesson. If the

---

[45] Exodus 40:34-35

children of Israel remembered Who carried them out of bondage, looking only to Him; if they listened and did as He required of them; if they watched over His covenant to do it, then they would be a peculiar treasure to God, above all people; and they'd be a *kingdom of priests* and a holy nation. That was God's goal for them! They, however, chose other things!

Now, under the Covenant of the Law, the priesthood shifted from a practice of a priesthood within the parameters of a chosen nation, to a select group who would sacrifice upon a newly defined and very specific altar. The sacrifices now were only accepted as offered through one tribe of priests alone, namely the offspring of Levi, beginning with a descendant named Aaron.

Here, through this lineage, God birthed the Aaronic order. At the same time, God ended the priesthood of the Patriarchs, which be began with Adam. That priesthood, unfortunately, was defiled by the priests who abandoned their proper loyalty to the living God and participated in the rites and rituals of the golden calf.

ABOUT THE SHIFT OF PRIESTHOOD

In looking at the shift of priesthood, remember *the nation of priests* that God desired to serve Him after the Exodus from Egypt, *did not happen.* If it had, there would be no need for the Aaronic order, under the Law. Yet, God's mercy prevailed over man's inability to understand God's greater plan. In God's mercy and love, He established that Aaronic order.

YeHoVaH's desire for a nation of priests, which was never again referred to within the First Covenant setting, would wait until a very different setting and circumstances, within the framework and power of the New Covenant, through His Son's blood:

1 Peter 2:5

> 5 Ye also, as lively stones, are built up a spiritual house, an holy priesthood, to offer up spiritual sacrifices, acceptable to God by Jesus Messiah.

1 Peter 2:9

> 9 But ye are a chosen generation, a royal priesthood, an holy nation, a peculiar people; that ye should shew forth the praises of him who hath called you out of darkness into his marvellous light:

Revelation 1:4-6

> 4 John to the seven churches which are in Asia: Grace be unto you, and peace, from him which is, and which was, and which is to come; and from the seven Spirits which are before his throne; 5 And from Jesus

Messiah, who is the faithful witness, and the first begotten of the dead, and the prince of the kings of the earth. Unto him that loved us, and washed us from our sins in his own blood, **6 And hath made us kings and priests unto God and his Father; to him be glory and dominion for ever and ever. Amen**[46].

Reading this, in 1 Peter and in Revelation, we see the priesthood of the believer is both one of a nation of priests and a royal priesthood. It is as John, the author of Revelation wrote so beautifully, kings and priests unto God! Through the cross, God received what could not be done under the Law! Through Yeshua's perfect sacrifice, YeHoVaH received that kingdom of priests and a holy nation!

A PERSONAL REFLECTION

Considering the kingdom of priests and holy nation, dear reader, *do you live a holy life?* You are positionally sanctified through the blood of Yeshua; however, you might think about the New Covenant's focus to align life's choices with God's idea of a holy lifestyle! You may ask the question, can a true born again believer defile their priesthood with a form of idolatry, as did those worshippers of the golden calf? Take some time, here, dear one and ask

---

[46] Bold and italics added by the author.

YeHoVaH! May He grant you eyes to see and ears to hear what His Spirit is saying!

A Chosen Lineage 5

As we saw in the last chapter entitled, "A Kingdom of Priests", YeHoVaH inaugurated the Aaronic priesthood, thus, shifting away from the former priesthood, which existed from the time of Adam. To ensure we understand the connection in the Aaronic priesthood to Abraham, the Father of all who came out of Egypt, we'll quickly look at the lineage of the Aaronic priesthood. Then, we'll investigate a rebellion that challenged God's choice of priesthood in the Covenant of the Law.

In investigating Aaronic lineage, let's open the early pages of Exodus. There we'll find a lineage listed as descending from Jacob, a descendant Abraham.⁴⁷ In the opening verses of Chapter One, we see written the names of the sons of Jacob and their families. These came into Egypt during the famine, during the time when Jacob discovered Joseph, his missing son supposed dead, was alive and well in Egypt. In fact, Joseph was a powerful leader in Egypt, second only to the Pharaoh.

Under the leadership of Jacob, and at the invitation of Pharaoh obtained through Joseph, the children of Israel entered Egypt.

Exodus 1:1-6

> "1 Now these are the names of the children of Israel, which came into Egypt; every man and his household came with Jacob. 2 Reuben, Simeon, Levi, and Judah, 3 Issachar, Zebulun, and Benjamin, 4 Dan, and Naphtali, Gad, and Asher. 5 And all the souls that came out of the loins of Jacob were seventy souls: for Joseph was in Egypt already. 6 And Joseph died, and all his brethren, and all that generation."

Lineage as we see recorded here, clearly designated those who came into Egypt, listing them as the sons of Jacob, (Abraham's grandson) whose name God changed to Israel.

---

⁴⁷ From Abraham came Isaac. From Isaac came Jacob.

As Israel's children greatly increased in number in Egypt, each family grew so large in number they became tribes. One tribe, of which we take great consideration, is the tribe of Levi. From *Levi's tribe* came many children, two of them important to the topic of this book, namely *Moses and Aaron*.

MOSES

Moses was God's chosen vessel commissioned to bring the children of Israel out of Egypt. Moses, in fulfilling that call, confronted Pharaoh, demanding a release of God's People. Moses also inaugurated the first Passover, and with God by his side, saw the deliverance of the children of Israel from the wicked Pharaoh, who enslaved them.

After their deliverance, Moses brings the entire nation to Mt. Sinai. As you saw in the last chapter, Moses was instrumental in receiving the 10 commandments for God's People. Moses, in his times with God upon Mt. Sinai, having seen God's Tabernacle, oversees the making and erection of a copy of that tabernacle upon the earth.

That Tabernacle, with all its elaborate draperies and golden furniture, became the place where a visible presence of God manifested. We call that Presence the Glory of YeHoVaH!

Exodus 40:33-38

> 33 And he (Moses) reared up the court round about the tabernacle and the altar, and set up the hanging of the court gate. So Moses finished the work. 34 Then a cloud covered the tent of the congregation, and the glory of YeHoVaH filled the tabernacle.
>
> 35 And Moses was not able to enter into the tent of the congregation, because the cloud abode thereon, and the glory of YeHoVaH filled the tabernacle. 36 And when the cloud was taken up from over the tabernacle, the children of Israel went onward in all their journeys:
>
> 37 But if the cloud were not taken up, then they journeyed not till the day that it was taken up. 38 For the cloud of YeHoVaH was upon the tabernacle by day, and fire was on it by night, in the sight of all the house of Israel, throughout all their journeys.

AARON

Aaron, a descendant of Abraham, received God's direct appointment to become High Priest[48] over God's Tabernacle, (God's house

---

[48] Exodus 28:1 "1 And take thou unto thee Aaron thy brother, and his sons with him, from among the children of Israel, that he may minister

which Moses oversaw and erected). Aaron formed the foundation of the Aaronic priesthood. As we discussed in the last chapter, the priesthood with Aaron shifted from the Adamic priesthood where heads of families were priests and the firstborn of families were High Priest.

 *With God's action of choosing Aaron, the high priest lineage changed from firstborn son, to the firstborn nation, namely Israel.*

While every father in the households of the children of Israel retained responsibilities for their family, their priestly office for sacrificial offerings, **God no longer accepted**. Sacrifices and offerings became the responsibility of Aaron and his sons, as God appointed. Later, we'll see how this change of priesthood was not accepted by some of the lineage of Levi. They grumbled that Moses and Aaron took many honours unto themselves.

No matter how man looked at it, however, God saw Aaron as the High Priest of His choice, *operative in the Covenant of the Law, immediately after the Law was given.* In his office, as High Priest of Israel, he offered sacrifices and

---

unto me in the priest's office, even Aaron, Nadab and Abihu, Eleazar and Ithamar, Aaron's sons."

offerings, as well as many other duties including intercession. We see the latter operative in a situation when God's righteous hand of judgment came upon the children of Israel. At that time, by Aaron's and Moses' action of intercession, many were spared from death.

KORAH'S REBELLION

In looking at Korah's rebellion, keep in mind the shifted priesthood, which moved from the "firstborn son" to the lineage of Aaron. This is an important factor, as certain people amongst the children of Israel *did not see* God's Hand in the direct change of priesthood. Consequently, their actions, which were rebellious against God's chosen order, proved as rebellion against God, Himself.

Turning our attention to Korah now, we see he originated from the tribe of Levi[49]. Korah, in his organized rebellion, attached himself to two other ringleaders, Dathan and Abiram. Dathan and Abiram were descendants from the tribe of Reuben, Jacob's firstborn son. These three men,

---

[49] Levi was the third son of Leah, first wife to Jacob. She became Jacob's first wife due to a means of deception, whereby Jacob thought she was his promised bride, Rebekah.

together with others, rebelled against Moses and Aaron:

Numbers 16:1-3

> 1 Now Korah, the son of Izhar, the son of Kohath, the son of Levi, and Dathan and Abiram, the sons of Eliab, and On, the son of Peleth, sons of Reuben, took men: 2 And they rose up before Moses, with certain of the children of Israel, two hundred and fifty princes of the assembly, famous in the congregation, men of renown: 3 And they gathered themselves together against Moses and against Aaron, and said unto them, Ye take too much upon you, seeing all the congregation are holy, every one of them, and YeHoVaH is among them: wherefore then lift ye up yourselves above the congregation of YeHoVaH?

We see from this scripture a complaint against Moses and Aaron, who in the opinion of Korah and his rebellious entourage, thought the two leaders took too much upon themselves. In their mind, they thought that every one of the children of Israel were holy and to prove their theory, they pointed out that YeHoVaH dwelt in their midst.

Moses first speaks directly to Korah and gives him a test for the next day, one whereby

YeHoVaH will prove to all who are the ones that are holy in God's eyes.

Numbers 16:6-7

> 6 This do; Take you censers, Korah, and all his company; 7 And put fire therein, and put incense in them before YeHoVaH to morrow: and it shall be that the man whom YeHoVaH doth choose, he shall be holy: ye take too much upon you, ye sons of Levi.

It is interesting to note, that comment of Moses was identical to the accusation of Korah, "you take too much upon you!" Moses then goes on with his comments explaining to Korah the good thing that God had already done for him and his family. God separated them out to do the service of the Tabernacle. That is a great honour giving them permission to minister before the congregation.

Numbers 16:8-9

> 8 And Moses said unto Korah, Hear, I pray you, ye sons of Levi: 9 Seemeth it but a small thing unto you, that the God of Israel hath separated you from the congregation of Israel, to bring you near to himself to do the service of the tabernacle of YeHoVaH, and to stand before the congregation to minister unto them?

Moses points out also, the good thing God has done to his brothers, the sons of Levi:

Numbers 16:10-11

> 10 And he hath brought thee near to him, and all thy brethren the sons of Levi with thee: and seek ye the priesthood also? 11 For which cause both thou and all thy company are gathered together against YeHoVaH: and what is Aaron, that ye murmur against him?

Moses puts the argument right in front and states it like it is! This is a cause against the choice of God, not of man. Why then, he asks, do you murmur at Aaron?

Leaving the test with Korah set for the next day, Moses sends to speak with Dathan and Abiram. However, they will not come up and speak with Moses. Instead, they send a complaint, accusing Moses of not keeping them alive in the desert for their sakes but his, so he could lord himself over them.

Moreover, they said that Moses did not bring them into a land flowing with milk and honey as promised, but rather to the burning sands of the desert. They asked Moses if he would now come and put their eyes out, so they wouldn't see what is happening, nor complain about it?

Moses, very angry with them, asks YeHoVaH not to respect their offering. In his own defence, Moses tells YeHoVaH that he did not take even as much as an ass from those people, nor has he hurt one of them!

Moses returns his comments to Korah, regarding the test tomorrow. Moses tells them:

Numbers 16: 16-17

> 16 And Moses said unto Korah, Be thou and all thy company before YeHoVaH, thou, and they, and Aaron, to morrow: 17 And take every man his censer, and put incense in them, and bring ye before YeHoVaH every man his censer, two hundred and fifty censers; thou also, and Aaron, each of you his censer.

On the next day, when Korah and his company of 250 princes took their censers with fire and incense added, they stood in the doorway of the tabernacle of the congregation with Moses and Aaron. As they stood there, the glory of YeHoVaH appeared unto all the congregation. With the glory of God near, YeHoVaH speaks to Moses and Aaron:

Numbers 16:21

> 21 Separate yourselves from among this congregation, that I may consume them in a moment

God made His choice! He stood with Moses and Aaron! Immediately, however, Moses and Aaron seek mercy:

Numbers 16:22

> 22 And they fell upon their faces, and said, O God, the God of the spirits of all flesh, shall one man sin, and wilt thou be wroth with all the congregation?

In response to this intercession, YeHoVaH tells Moses to instruct the people to get away from the tents of Korah, Dathan, and Abiram. He does so, advising them to touch none of their things. As the children of Israel moved away from the tents, Korah, Dathan, and Abiram, these men came out and stood in the door of their tents, along with their wives, sons, and little children.

Moses then makes this judgment:

Numbers 16: 28-30

> 28 And Moses said, Hereby ye shall know that YeHoVaH hath sent me to do all these works; for I have not done them of mine own mind. 29 If these men die the common death of all men, or if they be

visited after the visitation of all men; then YeHoVaH hath not sent me. 30 But if YeHoVaH make a new thing, and the earth open her mouth, and swallow them up, with all that appertain unto them, and they go down quick into the pit; then ye shall understand that these men have provoked YeHoVaH.

Sure enough, the ground opened its mouth and swallowed Korah, Dathan, and Abiram, as well their families, goods and people that stood with them. Those nearby fled in fear, but the 250 princes were consumed by a fire, which came out from YeHoVaH. It thus consumed those who had offered incense.

LESSONS FROM KORAH'S REBELLION

An immediate lesson comes to mind:

Agree with God in His choices of leadership.

However, there are deeper lessons here. Some, we'll see later, however, for now, let's remember that Korah, Dathan, and Abiram and those who rebelled with them, saw only the natural things of man, their own want, and their own craving for importance.

These men possessed a different mindset regarding a leadership position. Their mindset embraced not a servant-like mentality, as God required. They did not see God's Hand in the matter at hand, and from the records of the event, we see they did not seek God from a truly humble heart to learn God's truth.

Rather, they supposed their thoughts, their opinions, and even their former religious training was correct. These people sought not the mind of YeHoVaH. God, in His Sovereignty, has the right to appoint times and seasons, and to change them as He sees fit[50]. He rightfully decides who comes to minister to Him and how. He decides and chooses leadership, both spiritual and natural.

God's people can rest in that fact, and should they not agree with a chosen leader, they are free to humbly come, seek His face for help. Also, in their words and prayers for such leaders, grumbling has best be forgotten! It is far better to exchange the ideas of man, those which do not hold God's understanding, than to act in a manner considered rebellious against YeHoVaH.

For New Covenant believers, we need not fear the earth swallowing us up, as that is First Covenant; however, we can learn from this incident. We can learn to seek the mind of YeHoVaH, in all things, and not to treasure the things of the earth. That lesson, Yeshua taught

---

[50] Daniel 2:21-22

us Himself! We see that as Peter, the Apostle, rebuked Yeshua for His prophecy of going to the cross. As Yeshua addressed the issue, He rebuked ha satan and then added, "you savour not the things that are of God, but those that be of men."[51]

As we look at anything in our life, in our city, in our nation or other nations, too, it is always good to seek YeHoVaH as to what He is saying and doing. In today's information age, when people constantly present others with their assessment of situations, with their point of view and ideas on how things need to be resolved, while it may be difficult, believer's need to take their viewpoint from YeHoVaH!

We need to approach all topics, especially regarding individuals who God puts in places of authority, inside or outside of the Body of Messiah, with an attitude to seek God for His wisdom. In doing these things, our responses glorify God. Dear one, let's ensure we take a lesson from Korah's rebellion.

Let's learn to look to God for His choices, especially when it disagrees with the status quo, or our own wisdom.

---

[51] Matthew 16:23

Let's learn not to measure the things before our face with a measuring stick other than that of God's! May our heart, mind and spirit savour the things of God!

Aaronic Priesthood Tabernacle Part 1

6

One might wonder why God, during the time of Moses and Aaron, was so very rigid and strict regarding the making, erection and operation of the Tabernacle, the place where He chose to dwell with His people. We easily conclude that God's reasons embrace giving humankind insights to understanding Him, as well as what He desired in a relationship with His people.

As we investigate the setup of that tabernacle, with its sacrificial system, its moral codes of behaviour as well as its specific priesthood, we know God's messages are precise and direct, regarding any kind of an approach to Him. Fallen man, in looking at the careful and meticulous approach to the God of Abraham, Isaac and Jacob recognizes that the primary barrier between humankind and His creator is none other than the sin factor, which stands in direct contrast to the holiness of God. Man, in learning to deal with this sin factor, has invented many approaches to God. However, each one fails and will continue to fail until man agrees to do things God's way.

For some, this statement to do things God's way seems fair, considering we are dealing with the One who created the universe. To others, however, especially those who argue against His existence, it seems ridiculous. In looking at the Tabernacle, which was a reality, and at its definite and clearly laid out approach to God, precise spiritual truths about God are attainable. Here, we'll take the time to look at one or two of those truths[52].

THE TABERNACLE'S OUTWARD MESSAGE

On the outside, the Tabernacle of Moses, along with every aspect of its worship system, God defined a clear and disciplined approach to His Throne and to His person. The entire set up, with its inner and outer courts, its fences,

---

[52] Unfortunately, this topic requires a lot of time to explore in detail. We do not have time to do so here, however, there are many good studies available for you to explore.

pillars, hangings, roof and furniture speak on how to approach God while on earth and how to live with Him eternally. This Tabernacle of Moses clearly defined certain unavoidable respects for God, outlining His holiness and His desire to allow only that which is holy to draw near to Him. Such holiness of God required not only a careful approach to honour Him, but also presented a message on how to ensure one survived the experience!

That brings us to the sin factor. In approaching a holy God, as the Tabernacle's lessons teach, the sin factor prevents fellowship with the One Who is totally righteous in all His ways. Sin must be handled God's way and God's way alone! Failure to deal with sin, as God demands, means trying to come into a relationship with God on our terms, and not on His. This approach exalts the flesh. It stretches the wisdom of man to its limits and in doing so, rejects the wisdom of God. Lessons from the Tabernacle teaches us the ways of God so we may understand, learn and adopt them into our lives.

SIN OFFERING

Referring to the sin offering outlined in the First Covenant, the book of Hebrews gives us a clear shortcut to see one major truth of the Tabernacle. It picks up from the truth of God's desire for sin offerings for man's sake to approach Him, yet it goes deeper to the performance of His will! That obedience brings one to a point of salvation, which includes true repentance for sin. Hebrews speaks of the acceptable sin offering, from God's viewpoint, as well as the aspect of a truly repented heart:

Hebrews 10:1-4

> 1 For the law having a shadow of good things to come, and not the very image of the things, can never with those sacrifices which they offered year by year continually make the comers thereunto perfect. 2 For then would they not have ceased to be offered? because that the worshippers once purged should have had no more conscience of sins. 3 But in those sacrifices there is a remembrance again made of sins every year. 4 For it is not possible that the blood of bulls and of goats should take away sins.

Discussing the Law as having a "shadow" of good things to come, the author of Hebrews points out that the Tabernacle offered truths concealed in shadows. A shadow does not give great clarity to the object which casts the shadow. It points to it, and thus, if a person wishes to see the substance of that shadow, they look to the real thing. They by-pass the shadow and grab hold of the original!

In the case of the sacrifices for sin, the book of Hebrews says they were a shadow of the real thing. We know that real thing to be Yeshua, Who made Himself an offering for sin. This fits well with what the prophet Isaiah, who is speaking of Messiah said,

Isaiah 53:1-5

> "1 Who hath believed our report? and to whom is the arm of YeHoVaH revealed? 2 For he shall grow up before him as a tender plant, and as a root out of a dry ground: he hath no form nor comeliness; and when we shall see him, [there is] no beauty that we should desire him. 3 He is despised and rejected of men; a man of sorrows, and acquainted with grief: and we hid as it were [our] faces from him; he was despised, and we esteemed him not. 4 Surely he hath borne our griefs, and carried our sorrows: yet we did esteem him stricken, smitten of God, and afflicted. 5 But he [was] wounded for our transgressions, [he was] bruised for our iniquities: the chastisement of our peace [was] upon him; and with his stripes we are healed.

Isaiah lists more details which only seem to fit Yeshua, then he says of the Messiah:

Isaiah 53:10

> 10 Yet it pleased YeHoVaH to bruise him; he hath put [him] to grief: when thou shalt make his soul an offering for sin, he shall see [his] seed, he shall prolong [his] days, and the pleasure of YeHoVaH shall prosper in his hand."

Here we see the Messiah, Himself, became a sin offering. Picking up on that same thing, the author of Hebrews writes:

Hebrews 10:5-7

> 5 Wherefore when he cometh into the world, he saith, Sacrifice and offering thou wouldest not, but a body hast thou prepared me: 6 In burnt offerings and sacrifices for sin thou hast had no pleasure. 7 ¶ Then said I, Lo, I come (in the volume of the book it is written of me,[53]) to do thy will, O God.

Yeshua came in the book written of Him, namely the Hebraic scriptures. These speak of His conception by a virgin, His life as a Prophet and the Messiah, His death, burial and

---

[53] The author of Hebrews quotes the Psalmist here: Psalm 40:7

resurrection. Therefore, Yeshua said, "Look! I come in the volume of the book written of me to do Your will, O God"

In keeping with the topic of "sacrifice and offerings" from verse 6, the author of Hebrews adds, speaking in the first person for Yeshua:

Hebrews 10:8-10

> 8 Above when he said, Sacrifice and offering and burnt offerings and offering for sin thou wouldest not, neither hadst pleasure therein; which are offered by the law. 9 Then said he, Lo, I come to do thy will, O God. He taketh away the first, that he may establish the second. 10 By the which will we are sanctified through the offering of the body of Jesus Messiah once for all.

By these words, *"He takes away the first to establish the second, By the which will we are sanctified through the offering of the Body of Jesus Messiah once for all"*, we see the author of Hebrews shows Yeshua as the fulfilment of the Law and the Prophets.

With the Law being fulfilled, there is therefore now no need for sin-offerings to be offered any longer. That "sin-offering" which came at the first, is now removed because of the offering of Yeshua, once and for all.

Let's pick it up again in Hebrews:

Hebrews 10:11-14

> 11 And every priest standeth daily ministering and offering oftentimes the same sacrifices, which can never take away sins: 12 But this man, after he had offered one sacrifice for sins for ever, sat down on the right hand of God; 13 From henceforth expecting till his enemies be made his footstool. 14 For by one offering he hath perfected for ever them that are sanctified.

Here, from the book of Hebrews, we have a perfect analysis and breakdown of one message within the Tabernacle. Knowing that, we move on to better things, for God no longer remembers the sins and iniquities of the ones who accept Messiah, by faith, as their personal Saviour.

Instead, we move on to serve the Living and true God! Should we need another witness besides Isaiah and the Psalmist, Hebrews gives us one more proof:

Hebrews 10:15-17

> 15 Whereof the Holy Ghost also is a witness to us: for after that he had said before, 16 This is the covenant that I will make with them after those days, saith YeHoVaH, I will put my laws into their

hearts, and in their minds will I write them;
17   And their sins and iniquities will I remember no more.⁵⁴

Now, showing another witness, Hebrews concludes, making this important point:

Hebrews 10:18

18   Now where remission of these is, there is no more offering for sin.

In unlocking the truths within the Tabernacle, the book of Hebrews shows us Messiah as the sin-offering. He shows us that Yeshua is the only way to the Father, which is the message the gate and other aspects of the Tabernacle conveyed.

THE TABERNACLE'S HIDDEN MESSAGE

This Tabernacle of Moses, as we can see, spoke clearly of Yeshua. Yeshua is the reality, while the Tabernacle is but a shadow. If one had time to do an entire study, they'd find that the reality, Yeshua, is seen in every article, every colour, every aspect of that Tabernacle, from beginning to end, as it shows how to approach God. The only way in, is through God's Only Begotten Son, Yeshua. He is Saviour and is seen in such as the sacrificial offering for sin. He is depicted as the only way for complete sanctification,

---

⁵⁴ Quotes from Jeremiah 31:33 and Ezekiel 36:26

shown in the vessels used for washing, called the laver. He is depicted in every pillar, every post in the fence and literally every aspect of the entire system, even in the Aaronic priesthood[55].

In short, without a detailed analysis of the Tabernacle and the system of the Law put in place at that time, the message showed man in very clear terms, how to approach God through a Saviour of His choosing. He is the glory of God!

John 1:14

> 14 And the Word was made flesh, and dwelt among us, (and we beheld his glory, the glory as of the only begotten of the Father,) full of grace and truth.

HOW THIS AFFECTS THE PRIESTHOOD

Such a change in "sacrifice" requires changes in the priesthood. This we'll look at in the last section of the book. It is here noted, because the change of sacrifice indeed requires many changes to the accompanying priesthood.

---

[55] This we will discuss later, showing Yeshua's High Priest over God's House after a far better order than that of the Aaronic Priesthood.

Aaronic Priesthood Tabernacle
Part 2

There are many other messages of delight to the New Covenant believer, hidden within the shadows of the Tabernacle operative in the time of Moses. One such message has to do with the fear of YeHoVaH and what that means in our world today. Let's look at it.

THE FEAR OF GOD

Over the last few centuries, many have taught that the fear of YeHoVaH is simply a "respect" for God. While the fact of respect is certainly present, the First Covenant message of fear of YeHoVaH holds a much greater treasure in understanding the ways of God. It seems, "fear of YeHoVaH" in our casual society, where anything goes and where everything is acceptable, many people, without even knowing it, sweep under the carpet what God has said and defined as "good".

Many call "evil" good and "good" evil! In doing that, without understanding their actions, they block and try to erase a pathway to knowing God on His terms. That, however, is the only way to know God! We must never presume that humankind, with all his increasing wisdom, modern inventions or broadened sense of love and passion for the downtrodden, can afford to consider themselves greater or wiser than the One who created the world and all in it!

Isaiah, the prophet, in his day ran into those who thought their opinion and their judgments on things would stand, even in the face of a final judgment. Without realizing it, they, like many people today, went down a dangerous path where the flesh excused man's behaviour and elevated man's ways above God's ways. In doing so, they walked away from good counsel and embraced bad:

Isaiah 5: 19-25

"19 That say, Let him make speed, and hasten his work, that we may see it: and let the counsel of the Holy One of Israel draw nigh and come, that we may know it! 20 Woe unto them that call evil good, and good evil; that put darkness for light, and light for darkness; that put bitter for sweet, and sweet for bitter! 21 Woe unto them that are wise in their own eyes, and prudent in their own sight! 22 Woe unto them that are mighty to drink wine, and men of strength to mingle strong drink: 23 Which justify the wicked for reward, and take away the righteousness of the righteous from him!

24 Therefore as the fire devoureth the stubble, and the flame consumeth the chaff, so their root shall be as rottenness, and their blossom shall go up as dust: because they have cast away the law of YeHoVaH of hosts, and despised the word of the Holy One of Israel. 25 Therefore is the anger of YeHoVaH kindled against his people, and he hath stretched forth his hand against them, and hath smitten them: and the hills did tremble, and their carcases were torn in the midst of the streets. For all this his

anger is not turned away, but his hand is stretched out still."

The result of this pathway, in accordance with God's Word, brings a fruit of death and not life.

Life, however, is what God wants all humankind to receive, therefore, He carefully laid out in His Word how to live, how to approach Him and the consequences of doing things one's own way. Many who reject or bury the consequences resulting from breaking God's laws, do so in total ignorance. Nevertheless, the Judge of all the earth still holds man accountable for their actions.

Thus, in knowing this factor about God, knowing about His holiness, knowing about His desire for man to follow the correct approach to God as He sets out, and knowing that He judges according to His own Laws, aims to help man live correctly, and enjoy a long time.

God still says today what Joshua, the son of Nun, declared to the entire nation of Israel:

Joshua 24:15

> "15 And if it seem evil unto you to serve YeHoVaH, choose you this day whom ye will serve; whether the gods which your fathers served that were on the other side of the flood, or the gods of the Amorites, in

whose land ye dwell: but as for me and my house, we will serve YeHoVaH."

THE TABERNACLE'S MESSAGE ON HEAVEN

Next, the Tabernacle spoke of heaven, of God's Kingdom and how it operated. God, in His Own Kingdom operates within His only defined parameters of government. God is a Sovereign ruler of His Kingdom. His Kingdom is an effective and powerful Kingdom with armies, weaponry, and an amazing ability to rule in the Kingdom of men. The latter, however, is the choice of every person, as God neither forces His Kingdom on another, nor violates their free choice to live forever in darkness.

Heaven, in accordance with the layout of the Tabernacle, has only one entrance way. That is through the sacrificial blood of Yeshua, which He shed for all humankind on the cross of Calvary. There in only one requirement to enter past the gate and that fulfilling God's commandments, never failing once. We know this is impossible, however, Yeshua did that and as our Saviour, we receive His righteousness.[56]

---

[56] Romans 5: 17-21 "17 For if by one man's offence death reigned by one; much more they which receive abundance of grace and of the gift of righteousness shall

No one with sin may enter the Kingdom of God: Revelation 22:12-15

> "12 And, behold, I come quickly; and my reward is with me, to give every man according as his work shall be. 13 I am Alpha and Omega, the beginning and the end, the first and the last. 14 Blessed are they that do his commandments, that they may have right to the tree of life, and may enter in through the gates into the city. 15 For without are dogs, and sorcerers, and whoremongers, and murderers, and idolaters, and whosoever loveth and maketh a lie."

So much more is shown regarding heaven, in looking at the Tabernacle of Moses and God's system shown in the Hebraic scriptures. However, again, we don't have time to do an in-

---

reign in life by one, Jesus Messiah.) 18 Therefore as by the offence of one [judgment came] upon all men to condemnation; even so by the righteousness of one [the free gift came] upon all men unto justification of life. 19 For as by one man's disobedience many were made sinners, so by the obedience of one shall many be made righteous. 20 Moreover the law entered, that the offence might abound. But where sin abounded, grace did much more abound: 21 That as sin hath reigned unto death, even so might grace reign through righteousness unto eternal life by Jesus Messiah our Lord."

depth study on what heaven is like. For now, let's put our feet back on the ground! Let's take a quick look at governments we find operative upon the earth.

GOVERNMENTS IN OUR WORLD

There are many forms of government seen operative, worldwide. Some governments function with a self-appointed ruler who makes total decisions for all policies and procedures in that nation. Other forms of government function with an elected body of officials who do their best to bring about the best possible freedoms for the people of their nation.

Canada, falls more into the last category. Canada's form of government is called a Constitutional Monarchy, meaning Canada's government has a head of state, namely the ruling monarch or the United Kingdom, which at the time of this writing is Queen Elizabeth. Other nations who claim to operate as a Constitutional Monarchy are Belgium, Cambodia, Jordan, Norway, Spain, Sweden, and Thailand.

Each government in power over any nation, no matter the type, sets up rules and regulations which the people are expected to obey. Disobedience to laws have consequences. Some consequences are very severe, depending on the form of government operative in a nation. However, no matter the government in power, whether a nation admits it, or agrees to it, God holds that government, namely those in governmental positions of authority in their nation, responsible for the well-being or lack thereof, of its people. Again, whether nations admit to it or not, God also sets up kings (rulers) or sees them disposed!

Daniel 2:21-22

> "21 And he changeth the times and the seasons: he removeth kings, and setteth up kings: he giveth wisdom unto the wise, and knowledge to them that know understanding: 22 He revealeth the deep and secret things: he knoweth what [is] in the darkness, and the light dwelleth with him. "

When speaking of Governments, it is good to understand this, and this other fact also:

Psalm 103:19

> "19 ¶ The LORD hath prepared his throne in the heavens; and his kingdom ruleth over all."

Simply put, YeHoVaH is in charge, even if man does not acknowledge it, or even wish to agree to that fact! Therefore, as believers, keeping this thought in mind helps us to pray righteous prayers for those in governments, namely, that they do the will of YeHoVaH, for the sake of all!

1 Timothy 2:1-4

> "1 I exhort therefore, that, first of all, supplications, prayers, intercessions, and giving of thanks, be made for all men; 2 For kings, and for all that are in authority; that we may lead a quiet and peaceable life in all godliness and honesty. 3 For this is good and acceptable in the sight of God our Saviour; 4 Who will have all men to be saved, and to come unto the knowledge of the truth."

GOD'S GOVERNMENTAL RIGHTS

Recapping governments of earth, looking how they operate on the surface, we need to remember that God is still Sovereign. There are things that God will allow and things that He will not allow. There are times when God says over one kingdom, "you are finished", and whether they hear that Word of God, or not, it does not matter. That kingdom ends!

God rules over all.

When we recognize that fact, we can rest in it. We can take our peace knowing that even though we don't understand, God does. We also remind ourselves that we will never have the bigger picture!

No matter the government, no matter the time, no matter the world affairs or the events happening behind hidden doors that no one knows, God sees all, and He rules over all! God, Himself, has a much greater plan than any human being can even begin to dream.

God's bigness is incredible! His ability to bring about His plans and purposes, balanced with the free will He gives to man, is amazing! His justice and His fairness rule over all!

Psalm 89:14

"14 Justice and judgment are the habitation of thy throne: mercy and truth shall go before thy face."

Psalm 145:17

"17 The LORD is righteous in all his ways, and holy in all his works."

As far as the priesthood and duties therein, priests living under the First Covenant were commanded to present God's Word and truths in such a manner as to highlight the fear of YeHoVaH.

God expected a priest's exemplified behaviour to teach and demonstrate truth, thus portraying God's standards of holiness. Their entire lifestyle was to undoubtedly and distinctly, present to God and man that which is good and acceptable, while at the same time, shunning that which God finds offensive.

As the priest's example was seen by onlookers, that presentation of acceptability unto YeHoVaH, should point people directly to God's Kingdom standard as well as effect in this world. It should shine as a light to all those who wish to live by faith, to help them look past the everyday happenings of earth to see a Kingdom that is eternal and to a God who has the last say! To Him, we bow our knee and to Him we confess His Lordship!

Incense & Intercession 7

Exodus Chapter 30 gives us details of the Altar of Incense, located within the Tabernacle. As we read that passage, we see its location and its purpose:

Exodus 30:1-10

> 1 ¶ And thou shalt make an altar to burn incense upon: of shittim wood shalt thou make it. 2 A cubit shall be the length thereof, and a cubit the breadth thereof; foursquare shall it be: and two cubits shall be the height thereof: the horns thereof shall be of the same.

> 3 And thou shalt overlay it with pure gold, the top thereof, and the sides thereof round about, and the horns thereof; and thou shalt make unto it a crown of gold round

about. 4 And two golden rings shalt thou make to it under the crown of it, by the two corners thereof, upon the two sides of it shalt thou make it; and they shall be for places for the staves to bear it withal. 5 And thou shalt make the staves of shittim wood, and overlay them with gold.

6 And thou shalt put it before the vail that is by the ark of the testimony, before the mercy seat that is over the testimony, where I will meet with thee. 7 And Aaron shall burn thereon sweet incense every morning: when he dresseth the lamps, he shall burn incense upon it.

8 And when Aaron lighteth the lamps at even, he shall burn incense upon it, a perpetual incense before YeHoVaH throughout your generations. 9 Ye shall offer no strange incense thereon, nor burnt sacrifice, nor meat offering; neither shall ye pour drink offering thereon. 10 And Aaron shall make an atonement upon the horns of it once in a year with the blood of the sin offering of atonements: once in the year shall he make atonement upon it throughout your generations: it is most holy unto YeHoVaH.

This altar of incense, overlaid with gold, sat near the place where God defined His meeting place. Whenever Aaron lit the lamps, (the branches of the golden menorah), he was to burn a perpetual incense. From later portions of scripture, we know 4 main ingredients in the incense mixture:

Exodus 30:34

> 34 And YeHoVaH said unto Moses, Take unto thee sweet spices, stacte, and onycha, and galbanum; these sweet spices with pure frankincense: of each shall there be a like weight:

According to Jewish oral tradition, however, authorities believe there were eleven ingredients, not just four. No matter the mixture, however, it was prepared by an apothecary, and in its completed form, considered pure and holy.

This perfume mixture was never to be used for personal reasons, but always kept solely for the purposes of YeHoVaH. Anyone who thought they might like to make it for themselves, would be cut off from the people.

INCENSE AND INTERCESSION

After the rebellion of Korah, which we looked at in an earlier chapter, God made it very clear that He would not accept "strange fire". God gave instructions to Eleazar, the son of Aaron, to take up the censers of the 250 princes, whose incense offering God rejected. Eleazar was to take those censers of brass, and make broad plates for a covering of the altar. He said, these shall be a sign unto the children of Israel.

Numbers 16:39-40

> 39 And Eleazar the priest took the brazen censers, wherewith they that were burnt had offered; and they were made broad plates for a covering of the altar: 40 To be a memorial unto the children of Israel, that no stranger, which is not of the seed of Aaron, come near to offer incense before YeHoVaH; that he be not as Korah, and as his company: as YeHoVaH said to him by the hand of Moses.

Shortly, thereafter, the people murmured at Aaron and Moses, accusing them of killing the people of YeHoVaH.[57] As the people gathered together against Moses, they looked at the Tabernacle to see the cloud covered it and the glory of YeHoVaH appeared. YeHoVaH spoke to Moses. He told him to get out from amidst that gathering, for He would consume them in a moment.

Immediately, Moses and Aaron fell on their faces before YeHoVaH to intercede for this people. Moses says to Aaron to quick, take a

---

[57] Numbers 16:41-49

censer, and put fire in it from the brazen altar, then put incense on the coals.

Go, Moses said, to the congregation and make atonement for them. Moses knew the wrath of God had gone forth, and the form of that wrath was a plague.

Aaron immediately obeys the command of Moses. He ran into the midst of the congregation! The plague was there, amongst the people, so Aaron added the incense to the censer and made an atonement for the people.

Numbers 16: 48-49

> 48 And he stood between the dead and the living; and the plague was stayed. 49 Now they that died in the plague were fourteen thousand and seven hundred, beside them that died about the matter of Korah

AARON'S CENSER

Aaron, the High Priest acceptable before YeHoVaH, took fire, or coals in modern terms, from the brazen altar, which was the chosen altar of sacrifice ordained by God. Those coals from that sacrificial altar sat amongst the remnants from the brazen altar and its fire. On that altar, alone, were animal sacrifices performed, including sin offerings. Aaron, taking the coal or fire from the brazen altar meant that he has laid, as a base from which the incense burned, a holy and acceptable fire before God: *hot coals from off the altar!*

Aaron's actions, with the proper incense and fire, shows proper intercession made on behalf of the people. God immediately received this offering because Aaron acted within the requirements of God, as prescribed by God, Himself. Any other incense, *risen from any other coal or fire,* or used by any individual not assigned by God, such as those of Korah's, God *considered strange fire.*

However, that which is done within the guidelines God laid out, fall within the basis of a pleasing fragrance before YeHoVaH, and in this case, the specific incense brought specific results: God's hand of Judgment stayed.

GOD PROVES AARON'S PRIESTHOOD

With the plague now stayed, God gave orders to prove His choice of priesthood[58]. In that proving, God required everyone to cut a rod from a tree to represent their father's house. Twelve rods were cut, the names of the father (tribes) engraved upon it and presented to YeHoVaH. Each one was laid out before YeHoVaH.

---

[58] Numbers Chapter 17

God promised that one of those rods would bloom, and the one that did so shall show God's chosen priesthood. With this test, YeHoVaH set about to remove the grumbling against the priesthood of Aaron, once and for all. On the next day, Moses went into the tabernacle and brought out all the rods from before YeHoVaH.

As the people gathered round, Moses showed the rod with Aaron's name upon it. It budded, brought forth blossom and yielded almonds. Impossible for a dead branch! With the priesthood dispute now settled, YeHoVaH had Aaron's rod brought and kept in the ark of the testimony. It spoke as a token against the rebels who disagreed with God's choice of priesthood.

ALIGNING WITH GOD'S CHOICES

People, throughout many generations, have their opinions. When it comes to the things of YeHoVaH, however, man's opinions do not count! Man's own beliefs, judgments and the like carry no weight with God. Modern humankind does not like that fact! Modern humankind feels such ideas are archaic and certainly inapplicable to such an educated society. In thinking, in this manner, humankind aligns for trouble. It is better for us to look at the Word of God, what He says and what He holds as true!

God's Word is full of revelations to help us learn what He accepts. His Kingdom, His required behaviours and the like, are laid out so we know what He finds acceptable. Knowing, therefore, how specific God is, in showing us His Kingdom through the various aspects of the Word, especially through the revelation in the Tabernacle of Moses and its accompanying Law, we see how important it is *to understand the lineage of the priesthood, that which God chose, not man!*

Looking at the Aaronic priesthood helps us see God's chosen lineage happened for reasons. That lineage spoke of certain things, the sum of which we should take note or highlight in order to grasp the truths of the scriptures, to see God's bottom line. Regarding the priesthood, the bottom line is that, in the time of Moses, God displayed His glory through the Tabernacle, showing us the importance of doing things God's way. Moses was commanded to do things God's way when he set up the tabernacle!

Hebrews 8:5

> "5 Who serve unto the example and shadow of heavenly things, as Moses was admonished of God when he was about to make the tabernacle: for, See, saith he, that thou make all things according to the pattern shewed to thee in the mount."

Should we do anything less than Moses? Should we not do things God's Ways, too?

By looking at the lineage of Aaron, we see the need to align with God's choices and not our own. When we look at Aaron, recognizing that he was chosen by God, *and for that season*, we see a finger pointed to God's sovereign right to decide who ministers to Him and how!

We also see those who He declares may draw near to Him and by what specific means. In complying with God's requests, we don't just exemplify God's choices and decisions, rather, we respect them, and we take a lesson from them.

This might not seem important to some, or to others it may seem an obvious thing; however, in our society, today, there are people who take on things for themselves, such as certain honours, and even certain liberties proclaiming their message is true, even elevate it above God's message. Some people even declare they represent whole groups of people, when in fact, they do no such thing.

Many voices in our world, today, prove out as self-appointed, speaking falsely, but presenting their words and viewpoint as truth. Some may or may not claim they speak for God, but in any case, if their message does not line up with God's Words, God has not sent them.

On that same line, many nations make laws which oppress the people, rob the poor and steal from the blind. Many leaders of nations dwell in luxury, basking in splendour while their people go hungry in the streets and cry aloud to God for help. Many try and silence those voices in their ears by excusing what they do as part of their right as leaders or rulers.

In today's world, it doesn't take much to look around and see things others do on their own, with their own initiative and 100% without God's instructions or approval. When we see these things, we need to stop!

- We need to take a good look at what the God of heaven and earth is truly saying!
- We need to put aside man's thoughts, man's ideals, man's ways and embrace the things of God!
- We need to look at how God operates and align with His Word for best results.

One clear message for all in God's choice of lineage through Aaron is this:

God's choice stands!

Mankind may dislike that fact and may even try to change, alter, adjust or fight it, but the fact remains, what God has said ... stands forever! He has the last word! In fact, He is the last word!

Revelation 21:6

> "6 And he said unto me, It is done. I am Alpha and Omega, the beginning and the end. I will give unto him that is athirst of the fountain of the water of life freely."

 **SECTION CONCLUSION**

In this book, thus far, we have mentioned two very specific priesthoods:

1. Those after the Adamic order, with priests such a Noah, and Abraham.[59]
2. The Aaronic Priesthood (that which comes through the lineage of Aaron, a descendant of Abraham.)

We've looked at these priesthoods for one major reason: *to see what was operative prior to the covenant made in Yeshua's blood*. Knowing that,

---

[59] Others operated in this priesthood too, ones we have not mentioned such as Enoch, Methuselah, Job, and even Isaac and Jacob.

helps us to compare Yeshua's covenant, with its priesthood, to that of Melchizedek. We see it is far better! As we now leave the first two sections behind us and move into the third section, we need to also leave behind our thinking about these two priesthoods.

For sure, there are lessons which we can learn from the two former orders of priesthood. We can glean from certain aspects of their lifestyle, altar, and sacrifice, as well as the tabernacle that accompanied the Aaronic priesthood. However, we need to come out from under the *shadow* of the original, to gaze full faced into the reality that cast that shadow! That which is perfect has come, (Yeshua!) and thus, the former altars, sacrifices and priesthoods pale in the light of the glory of His coming!

As the Adamic priesthood was no longer seen by God *as the operative priesthood* while the Tabernacle was erected, so too, **the Aaronic priesthood is no longer needed, for Yeshua has come!** After the cross, through what we call the 'New Covenant", **the priesthood in Messiah comes into full operation, functioning after the order of Melchizedek.**

Regarding the order of Melchizedek, we are told little in the book of Genesis, where the king, operating in that priesthood, first appears. At that time, we are told nothing of the king's origin, nor lineage. In the New Covenant, however, we are told it is the established priesthood of Yeshua, the Great High Priest of our New Covenant.

As we recognize that important fact, we recognize another shift in priesthood took place:

- Just as YeHoVaH installed the order of Aaron, and no longer accepted the Adamic order of priesthood, *we find that the Aaronic order is now ended, with the inauguration of the New Covenant.*
- As the New Covenant in Yeshua's blood came in, God moved forward with His plans and purposes, shifting the priesthood order to that of Melchizedek and so must we!

We must take a lesson from Korah, Dathan and Abiram and the 250 princes that died when they rebelled against God's priesthood shift in their time! *God's shift to a far greater priesthood must be followed by our obedience!* Otherwise, *we walk in rebellion.* Our thinking and behaviour must move forward to accept His change.

While these points may seem redundant to some, the fact is that, today, there is a revival in certain sectors of Christianity of the two former orders of priesthood, Adamic which some call, Patriarchal, and Aaronic, which many call, Levitical. **Neither of these** priesthoods belong to the New Covenant believer. [60]

Before closing this section, please examine your thinking, regarding the Apostolic Writings and the true priesthood of the believer. Examine your teachings regarding the priesthood. If you cling to the priesthood of Aaron or even the Adamic, ask YeHoVaH to open your eyes to see things His Way!

It is important, dear reader, that you believe and respond as the Apostolic Writings demand. Whether we know it or not, we have a responsibility *to both God and man* to get it right!

DO YOU LOVE ISRAEL?

Just as a point of mention, regarding getting the priesthood of the believer correctly, here is one very good reason for us to get it right today! You see, in Israel, even now as this book is written, there has been a mighty resurgence of the Aaronic order of priests. These priests have been carefully

---

[60] This should come clear as we walk through the next section, together.

selected from the Cohen tribe of Levites, that which they can detect by blood tests. Today, they have re-established the order, fashioning it carefully after the Aaronic order of priests found in the Torah (5 books of Moses). They have readied all the furniture and vessels, for the temple, to the exact dimensions, material and construction as commanded in the Torah. They have also re-installed their Sanhedrin.

In a moment's notice, they are ready to see their temple erected, dependent of course, on the platform of the Temple Mount, which they believe God will make available to them. Once they have their temple, they will re-instate animal sacrifices. To prepare for that day, they have what is called re-enactments.

In Jerusalem in 2016, such a re-enactment took place! Their reason is twofold. One is to prepare their Aaronic order of priests to function in their duties, and the other is to show the Gentiles in the world that they are ready for their Temple, and to invite them to offer sacrifices for the redemption of their souls!

This being the fact, we know we are not only close to Yeshua's return, we face a time when salvation to the Jews is imperative! They must learn to receive Yeshua, now! When they come to Messiah, those of us who have lived within the New Covenant framework need to ensure that *we not only accept God's changed order from Aaronic to Melchizedek, but live it out, functioning well in it!*

Jews, who come to Messiah at this point in history, need to grasp the fact that those in Messiah have *no need to partake in those re-established temple services,* and that their present priesthood in Messiah **is that of Melchizedek, not Aaron!** They need to see their priesthood in Messiah as the far greater order that God intended!

We need to teach it right

Oh, church!

We need to get it right!

We need to live it right!

COURSE 301

SECTION 3:

PRIESTHOOD

From the cross forward

A Change of Priesthood   8

In looking at the scriptures, we saw that the Aaronic priesthood began with Aaron, the brother of Moses. We saw its beginning within the timeframe of the Covenant of the Law, when God set up the sacrificial system.

Exodus 28:1

> 1 ¶ And take thou unto thee Aaron thy brother, and his sons with him, from among the children of Israel, that he may minister unto me in the priest's office, even Aaron, Nadab and Abihu, Eleazar and Ithamar, Aaron's sons.

Prior to this time, Aaron was chosen by God to be a spokesperson for Moses. Moses, when asked by God to speak to Pharaoh, felt thoroughly unable. Even all God's encouragement seemed not enough to move Moses to act on God's behalf. God, angry with Moses for his refusal, gave Aaron to Moses to speak to Pharaoh:

Exodus 4:14-17

> 14 And the anger of YeHoVaH was kindled against Moses, and he said, Is not Aaron the Levite thy brother? I know that he can speak well. And also, behold, he cometh forth to meet thee: and when he seeth thee, he will be glad in his heart. 15 And thou shalt speak unto him, and put words in his mouth: and I will be with thy mouth, and with his mouth, and will teach you what ye shall do.
>
> 16 And he shall be thy spokesman unto the people: and he shall be, even he shall be to thee instead of a mouth, and thou shalt be to him instead of God. 17 And thou shalt take this rod in thine hand, wherewith thou shalt do signs.

Aaron, in his task as speaking for Moses, God called a prophet:

Exodus 7:1

> 1 ¶ And YeHoVaH said unto Moses, See, I have made thee a god to Pharaoh: and Aaron thy brother shall be thy prophet.

Aaron operated as a prophet and a priest, and in his role within the Mosaic covenant foreshadowed the role of Messiah. However, something of the Messiah's priestly role was absent from the Aaronic priesthood!

REVIEW OF AARONIC PRIESTHOOD

Scripture devotes many pages and gives extensive details on the Aaronic order as it defines its specific lineage, its rites and rituals, altars and sacrifices, as well as details of service. Priests taught the people the commandments and other teachings of the Word of God. Some priests also operated in a prophetic office. *None, however, operated in the kingly role.* Only on one occasion do we see a High Priest, *momentarily crowned*,[61] and that was *to show the kingly role of the Messiah*.

Zechariah 6:11-14

> 11 Then take silver and gold, and make crowns, and set them upon the head of Joshua the son of Josedech, the high priest; 12 And speak unto him, saying, Thus speaketh YeHoVaH of hosts, saying, Behold the man whose name is The BRANCH; and he shall grow up out of his

---

[61] Zechariah Chapter 6

place, and he shall build the temple of YeHoVaH:

13 Even he shall build the temple of YeHoVaH; and he shall bear the glory, and shall sit and rule upon his throne; and he shall be a priest upon his throne: and the counsel of peace shall be between them both. 14 And the crowns shall be to Helem, and to Tobijah, and to Jedaiah, and to Hen the son of Zephaniah, for a memorial in the temple of YeHoVaH.

Aaron's position as High Priest was an extremely important and powerful position in many ways, including the fact that his role foreshadowed the Messiah; however, it did not foreshadow the Messiah's priestly role, *in its entirety!* This means the Aaronic priesthood did not foreshadow one of the most important roles of the Messiah, that of kingship!

FAILURE OF AARONIC PRIESTHOOD

Not only did the Aaronic priesthood not show the kingly role of the Messiah, but the Aaronic priesthood also had an unresolvable problem. That problem the book of Hebrews highlights:

Hebrews 7:11-14

11 If therefore perfection were by the Levitical priesthood, (for under it the people received the law,) what further

need was there that another priest should rise after the order of Melchisedec, and not be called after the order of Aaron? 12 For the priesthood being changed, there is made of necessity a change also of the law.

13 For he of whom these things are spoken pertaineth to another tribe, of which no man gave attendance at the altar. 14 For it is evident that our Lord sprang out of Juda; of which tribe Moses spake nothing concerning priesthood.

Hebrews 7 continues with this theme, adding this comment a few verses later:

Hebrews 7:19

19 For the law made nothing perfect, but the bringing in of a better hope did; by the which we draw nigh unto God.

In these few verses from Hebrews 7:11 to 19, we see that the Law could not make anyone perfect. Therefore, another priesthood was necessary! Of this perfection, Hebrews 9 also speaks. The author begins with the event of the Holy Spirit tearing the veil within the Temple:

Hebrews 9:8-11

> 8 The Holy Ghost this signifying, that the way into the holiest of all was not yet made manifest, while as the first tabernacle was yet standing: 9 Which [was] a figure for the time then present, in which were offered both gifts and sacrifices, that could ***not make him that did the service perfect***[62], as pertaining to the conscience; 10 [Which stood] only in meats and drinks, and divers washings, and carnal ordinances, imposed [on them] until the time of reformation.
>
> 11 But Messiah being come an high priest of good things to come, by a greater and more perfect tabernacle, not made with hands, that is to say, not of this building;

Hebrews speaks of the inability of the Aaronic order, with its ordinances, divine services and worldly sanctuary to change a person inwardly!

However, when the time of reformation had come, (the time when all things are realigned with God's Order), things changed. The far greater sacrifice of Yeshua, the spotless lamb of God, changed for all time the sacrifice as well as the priesthood. Clearly, Hebrews tells us that the blood of bulls and goats, as was operative within the Aaronic order, could not sanctify the

---

[62] Bold and italics the author's.

flesh. Only the blood of Yeshua can do that and through the priesthood of Yeshua, alone!

Hebrews 9:11-15

> 11 But Messiah being come an high priest of good things to come, by a greater and more perfect tabernacle, not made with hands, that is to say, not of this building; 12 Neither by the blood of goats and calves, but by his own blood he entered in once into the holy place, having obtained eternal redemption [for us].
>
> 13 For if the blood of bulls and of goats, and the ashes of an heifer sprinkling the unclean, sanctifieth to the purifying of the flesh: 14 How much more shall the blood of Messiah, who through the eternal Spirit offered himself without spot to God, purge your conscience from dead works to serve the living God?
>
> 15 ¶ And for this cause he is the mediator of the new testament, that by means of death, for the redemption of the transgressions [that were] under the first testament, they which are called might receive the promise of eternal inheritance."

Priesthood within the Aaronic parameters could not cleanse the conscience from dead works to serve a living God! For this reason,

Yeshua is the mediator of the New Covenant. Through His death, burial and resurrection, believers receive an eternal inheritance.

Is not this a far better priesthood? Does it not produce far better results?

THE PRIESTHOOD OF MELCHIZEDEK

Regarding the exact details of the priesthood of Melchizedek, we have little information. We are told that it was without lineage, without beginning and end, which information surely points to the eternal application of the priesthood to Yeshua.

Hebrews 7:12-16

> 12 For the priesthood being changed, there is made of necessity a change also of the law. 13 For he of whom these things are spoken pertaineth to another tribe, of which no man gave attendance at the altar. 14 For it is evident that our Lord sprang out of Juda; of which tribe Moses spake nothing concerning priesthood.
>
> 15 And it is yet far more evident: for that after the similitude of Melchisedec there ariseth another priest, 16 Who is made, not

after the law of a carnal commandment, but after the power of an endless life.

Yeshua's priesthood never ends, unlike the Aaronic priesthood. When a priest under that order died, they no longer functioned in their role. Yeshua, however, risen from the dead and seated at the Father's right hand, has an endless life. His position as High Priest after the order of Melchizedek will never end!

Hebrews 7:17

> 17 For he testifieth, Thou art a priest for ever after the order of Melchisedec.

Yeshua, the Messiah, was confirmed into His priesthood by an oath from God. No other office of priesthood came in with an oath: not the Adamic and not the Aaronic. Likewise, the Adamic and Aaronic had a destined end by God. Yeshua's priesthood, however, will neither change nor fade away. It is a continuous priesthood! His priesthood, also, avails to all who draw near to Him in truth:

Hebrews 7:25

> "Wherefore he is able also to save them to the uttermost that come unto God by him, seeing he ever liveth to make intercession for them."

APPLICATION TO BELIEVERS

What does all this mean to believers in Messiah? What might seem shocking to many believers, *(especially to those who have been taught otherwise)*, it sets a precedence for believers to recognize that they have a priesthood, and it connects directly and intimately with that of Messiah's.

Revelation 1:5-6

> "5 And from Jesus Messiah, who is the faithful witness, and the first begotten of the dead, and the prince of the kings of the earth. Unto him that loved us, and washed us from our sins in his own blood, 6 And hath made us ***kings and priests***[63] unto God and his Father; to him be glory and dominion for ever and ever. Amen.

This passage which says, *"washed us from our sins in his own blood"*, refers to born again believers, those who are fully incorporated by faith into the blood covenant in Messiah. The only priestly order in the Bible, which clearly speaks of a priesthood ***as king and priests***, is that of Melchizedek. This passage in Revelation points its finger to discover the roots from which priesthood the believer operates.

---

[63] Bold and italics the authors.

In looking at Biblical priesthoods, we see the Aaronic priesthood, with many functions which have similarities to the priesthood of Melchizedek, *yet it was never a kingly order, nor does it abide forever!* It is clear, then, the only order to which Revelation refers is that of Melchizedek. Therefore, we see that believers **in Messiah** stem ***not from the Aaronic order,*** as has been taught for many years, but rather from the order of kings and priests.

Understanding the difference between the Melchizedek and Aaronic priesthood, then, should bring much light to the believer. Knowing to which order we belong helps to better understand the role, more specifically. Anyone struggling with this thought, might ask themselves this question: "In accordance with scripture, those operating in the New Covenant do so in a far better covenant, so why not, a far better priesthood?"

Moving into that new mindset may seem difficult for some, however, if you think about it, it makes perfect biblical sense:

- We are in a far better covenant.[64]

---

[64] Hebrews 8:6 But now hath he obtained a more excellent ministry, by how much also he is the mediator of a better covenant, which was established upon better promises.

- We are joined to Messiah, being baptized into His death, burial, and resurrection.
- We are seated with Him in heavenly places.

Why then, would we operate in the manner of the Aaronic (Levitical) priesthood? It only follows that our order of priesthood follows that of Yeshua and subsequently, so would our lifestyle, as we live as priests unto God. Would it not, therefore, be more biblically accurate to say we operate in the same priesthood as our Lord and Master, Yeshua?

As we learn to think in line with *the proper* priesthood that is the believer's *in Messiah*, then, one is better equipped to live it out to the fullest extent, embracing the proper altar, presenting the proper sacrifice, dispensing all required and privileged duties, as assigned by God, Almighty.

Knowing we are of this order, we'll investigate further what this means in living out our priesthood within our commitment to follow Yeshua. In the meantime, please make this change of priesthood and how it affects your life, a matter of prayer. Listen to what the Holy Spirit would say to you. In doing so, remember:

God gave believers, in Messiah,
A FAR BETTER COVENANT
would He not, therefore, also give believers
A FAR BETTER PRIESTHOOD?

A Change of Tabernacle
Part 1 — 9

When looking at the tabernacle from where our Yeshua operates in His role as High Priest, we must learn to think past the elements of the earth and raise our sights higher. However, since we are still upon the earth, how do we do that? Our answer lies in looking at the early tabernacle God gave to Moses, and from that layout, understand what God laid out in heaven.

THE PATTERN OF HEAVEN

Due to the tabernacle in the wilderness representing heaven, from which Aaron mediated as a High Priest, Moses was told by

YeHoVaH to be sure he made all things identical to what he saw on the mountain:

Hebrews 8:3-5

> 3 For every high priest is ordained to offer gifts and sacrifices: wherefore it is of necessity that this man have somewhat also to offer. *4 For if he were on earth, he should not be a priest, seeing that there are priests that offer gifts according to the law[65]:* 5 Who serve unto the example and shadow of heavenly things, as Moses was admonished of God when he was about to make the tabernacle: for, See, saith he, that thou make all things according to the pattern shewed to thee in the mount.

In this New Covenant example, we see God's admonition to Moses to ensure he did not deviate from what he saw of heaven's tabernacle. That meant Moses was not to add to it or to take away from it. We know from the Hebraic Scriptures, Moses did a good job because YeHoVaH was very pleased, so pleased in fact, that He filled that tabernacle with His glory:

---

[65] We'll come back to this verse, momentarily.

Exodus 40:33 b-35

> 33 b. So Moses finished the work. 34 Then a cloud covered the tent of the congregation, and the glory of YeHoVaH filled the tabernacle. 35 And Moses was not able to enter into the tent of the congregation, because the cloud abode thereon, and the glory of YeHoVaH filled the tabernacle.

EARTH'S PATTERN TRANSLATED

In looking at the Mosaic Tabernacle[66], earlier we spoke of the Aaronic order of priesthood. When investigating that order, it was mentioned that that tabernacle had its ordinances, many of which the High Priest performed. To grasp an understanding of the Heavenly Tabernacle, whereby Yeshua functions as the High Priest, we need to grasp His qualifications.

Our Apostolic scriptures, in explaining those qualifications, begin by showing Yeshua's lineage on earth. That lineage did not qualify Him for the High Priest job in heaven! Something else, therefore must qualify Him.

---

[66] Tabernacle Moses made and erected in the wilderness. Also called Tabernacle in the wilderness.

Hebrews 8:4-6

4 For if he were on earth, he should not be a priest, seeing that there are priests that offer gifts according to the law: 5 Who serve unto the example and shadow of heavenly things, as Moses was admonished of God when he was about to make the tabernacle: for, See, saith he, that thou make all things according to the pattern shewed to thee in the mount. 6 But now hath he obtained a more excellent ministry, by how much also he is the mediator of a better covenant, which was established upon better promises.

Yeshua's tribe had nothing to do with the priesthood, yet we are told Yeshua has obtained a more excellent High Priest ministry than that of any other earthly ministry. What gave Yeshua the qualifications, in God's eyes to be the High Priest of this New Covenant? We'll find that answer by looking at a particularly important task of the High Priest: *making atonement for sin.*

MAKING AN ATONEMENT FOR SIN

Again, looking to the book of Hebrews, we have an excellent summary of the duties of the High Priest as he made atonement for sin.

Hebrews 9:1-5

> 1 Then verily the first covenant had also ordinances of divine service, and a worldly sanctuary. 2 For there was a tabernacle made; the first, wherein was the candlestick, and the table, and the shewbread; which is called the sanctuary. 3 And after the second veil, the tabernacle which is called the Holiest of all; 4 Which had the golden censer, and the Ark of the Covenant overlaid round about with gold, wherein was the golden pot that had manna, and Aaron's rod that budded, and the tables of the covenant; 5 And over it the cherubims of glory shadowing the mercyseat; of which we cannot now speak particularly.

Hebrews speaks of the two chambers within the tabernacle. The first chamber, which the author called a Sanctuary, held a candlestick and table of shewbread[67]. There was a veil that separated this chamber from the inner one, called the Holy of Holiest (Holiest of all). Within that chamber, says the author of Hebrews, stood the gold censer, the Ark of the Covenant. Inside the

---

[67] Some believe the altar of incense was in this area, while others believe it was inside with the ark. Hebrew's author believed it was in the inner chamber with the Ark of the Covenant.

chest like part of the ark, was the golden pot containing a sample of manna, Aaron's rod that budded,[68] and the tables of stone, wherein the Law was written. On top of the closed lid of the ark sat, what is called the "Mercy Seat", with cherubims of glory. Upon that Mercy Seat, the High Priest sprinkled blood from the sacrificial offering:

Hebrews 9:6-7

> 6 Now when these things were thus ordained, the priests went always into the first tabernacle, accomplishing the service of God. 7 But into the second went the high priest alone once every year, not without blood, which he offered for himself, and for the errors of the people:

Only the High Priest could enter the second chamber, the Holy of Holies, and at that, he must bring an offering of blood for sins. He must bring blood for his own sins and then for the sins of the people. In this action, there was a hidden message. That message Hebrews makes clear:

Hebrews 9: 8-10

> 8 The Holy Ghost this signifying, that the way into the holiest of all was not yet made

---

[68] We spoke of that in chapter Seven.

> manifest, while as the first tabernacle was yet standing: 9 Which was a figure for the time then present, in which were offered both gifts and sacrifices, that could not make him that did the service perfect, as pertaining to the conscience; 10 Which stood only in meats and drinks, and divers washings, and carnal ordinances, imposed on them until the time of reformation.

As the scriptures just related, the Holy Spirit, by originally setting up the veil which divided the outer and inner chamber, He showed all onlookers that the way into the very Presence of YeHoVaH was obscure. One factor, however, was very clear: *only the High Priest could enter, and only with the blood of the sacrifice for sins.* Then, on God's appointed day, He tore the veil.

Matthew 27:51[69]

> 51 And, behold, the veil of the temple was rent in twain from the top to the bottom; and the earth did quake, and the rocks rent;

That torn veil shows the way into the Holy of Holies. It is not through the blood sacrifices operative within the Aaronic priesthood. It is,

---

[69]Also recorded in two other gospels: *Mark 15:38 And the veil of the temple was rent in twain from the top to the bottom; Luke 23:45 And the sun was darkened, and the veil of the temple was rent in the midst.*

rather, through the blood of Yeshua, for that veil represented the flesh of Yeshua:

Hebrews 10:19-20

> 19 Having therefore, brethren, boldness to enter into the holiest by the blood of Jesus, 20 By a new and living way, which he hath consecrated for us, through the veil, that is to say, his flesh;

At that point, through the sacrifice of Yeshua, the tabernacle on earth became obsolete. It was a sign pointing to that which is perfect, and now, that which is perfect has come: "Yeshua, the perfect lamb of God, the perfect sacrifice".

This tabernacle of earth, with its outward expression, was imposed upon the people until the time of reformation. With Yeshua's sacrifice, the time of reformation had come. In other words, the entire system of worship as set up by Moses, shifted from its carnal ordinances and applications to spiritual. To understand the enormous effects of this one-time atonement, we need to examine the words *"a time of Reformation"*.

A TIME OF REFORMATION

Before looking at the Heavenly Tabernacle in greater detail, let's take a sidestep. Let's look at the word, "Reformation" in Hebrews 9:10 (see in the previous scripture).

Reformation	Greek #1357
διόρθωσις	Pronounced *dee-or'-tho-sis*
This is a compound word, meaning to thoroughly straighten. In a physical sense, it makes something straight that was out of alignment	

If we put this meaning into the scriptural sentence from which it came, it reads like this:

Hebrews 9:10 paraphrased

> 10 *(In reference to Mosaic Tabernacle and all its components) these,* "stood only in meats and drinks, and divers washings, and carnal ordinances, imposed on them until the time of when *all things came back into alignment with God's order.*

WHAT WAS OUT OF ALIGNMENT

Before the cross, what was out of alignment? To answer that question, we shift back to Adam. When Adam did not watch, as commanded by God, when he did not subdue ha satan (the adversary), he sinned and opened the door to death. "Death" was never God's plan for humankind. God designed humankind to bear His image and live eternally with Him.

"Death", was not in alignment! Death needed to be removed. It can only be removed with atonement for sin. Under the First Covenant, that atonement pointed to the Heavenly Tabernacle. That Heavenly Tabernacle, according to the book of Hebrews, must be purified with better things than the blood of animals:

Hebrews 9:23

> 23 It was therefore necessary that the patterns of things in the heavens should be purified with these; but the heavenly things themselves with better sacrifices than these.

Therefore, Messiah entered the Holy Place in Heaven's Tabernacle and appeared before the Presence of YeHoVaH on behalf of humankind[70]. Yet, unlike the High Priest on earth, He did not have to make atonement for His own sins, because He was sinless. That sinless blood cleansed the way, making it possible for humankind to enter eternal life with God.

"Death", the punishment for sin, is now conquered! That which was out of God's order, in man's world, is now made right. It is straightened! All who would live eternally, can

---

[70] Hebrews 9:23-28

do so by accepting the offering for sin made on their behalf. Now, He appeared at (*what the book of Hebrews call*) "the end of the world", to appear before God to put away sin, because it is appointed once for man to die and then judgment comes. Messiah then offered his blood on behalf of all who'd accept Him as their Lord and Saviour. Judgment for sin came upon Yeshua!

Looking at Yeshua's personal life, when judged, He was acquitted of any wrongdoing. His life was totally righteous, as the Judge of all the earth deemed it! His sinless blood, now in heaven, shows the open door to eternal life.

Picking this thought up from Hebrews 9, we read:

Hebrews 9:11-12

> 11 But Messiah being come an high priest of good things to come, by a greater and more perfect tabernacle, not made with hands, that is to say, not of this building; 12 Neither by the blood of goats and calves, but by his own blood he entered in once into the holy place, having obtained eternal redemption for us.

Messiah, even though He is not of any earthly order of priests, is a High Priest of good things to come. His service is in a greater tabernacle which is perfect. That tabernacle is not made with human hands! It is not of any building on earth. In addition, His precious blood cleansed all things, Hebrews goes on to say, where the blood of bulls and goats could not:

Hebrews 9:13-14

> 13 For if the blood of bulls and of goats, and the ashes of an heifer sprinkling the unclean, sanctifieth to the purifying of the flesh: 14 How much more shall the blood of Messiah, who through the eternal Spirit offered himself without spot to God, purge your conscience from dead works to serve the living God?

Here we see that the blood of Yeshua, sprinkled upon the believer, *cleanses his conscience* from dead works. The worshipper can now shift from dead works to serve a living God!

This is great news for the believer! As we come to Messiah, Yeshua's high priestly ministry takes effect as He sprinkles our conscience with His precious blood. That is one of His priestly duties, more of which we'll look at in another chapter.

A Change of Tabernacle
Part 2

From this Heavenly Tabernacle, Yeshua performs His duties as High Priest. He does so from a Heavenly Sanctuary that has all things in alignment! Nothing is out of order in God's tabernacle in Heaven! The time of "straightening", the time of "reformation" has come. Mankind, through the blood sacrifice of Yeshua's sinless blood, can now live forever!

Since this New Covenant is far greater, the New Covenant believer can also enjoy a conscience free from guilt of sin. In addition, there is a new heart implanted on which the Laws of God are written. Decisions made from that heart will align the believer to walk within the righteous Laws of God. If that were not enough, God has given even more! Man draws near to God and with the sin problem resolved, a wonderful and delightful relationship develops between God and His child.

Yeshua is indeed the mediator of a better covenant. That better covenant was established on much better promises:

Hebrews 8:7-8

> 7 For if that first covenant had been faultless, then should no place have been sought for the second. 8 For finding fault with them, he saith, Behold, the days come, saith YeHoVaH, when I will make a new covenant with the house of Israel and with the house of Judah:

One better promise which the New Covenant believer enjoys, is a never changing priesthood. On earth, under the Aaronic priesthood, men lived out their lifetime and then passed away. Another person took their place. In heaven, in this far better covenant, with better promises, we have a Great High Priest who lives forever! His role never ends, nor is it ever to be taken over by another. He has secured that role, forever!

More promises of the better covenant outshone the First Covenant, also, in terms of limitations and scope of its affect. For example, under the terms of the first covenant, along with its Aaronic priesthood, the sacrifices could not make the bearer perfect.[71] In other words, a repented believer, once saved by faith, *under the First Covenant,* was not *affected internally.* His or her heart, *(which remember in Hebraic thought is the place where decision making takes place)* was never changed. This change is incredibly important!

Laws within the Mosaic system were written on tablets of stone, and it was, therefore, an external covenant affecting one externally. However, the New Covenant in Yeshua's blood affects one internally, right at the source of the problem: *the heart.*

Hebrews 8:7-10

> 7 For if that first covenant had been faultless, then should no place have been sought for the second. 8 For finding fault with them, he saith, Behold, the days come, saith YeHoVaH, when I will make a new covenant with the house of Israel and with the house of Judah: 9 Not according to the covenant that I made with their fathers in the day when I took them by the hand to lead them out of the land of Egypt; because

---

[71] Hebrews 7:19 discussed in Chapter 7.

they continued not in my covenant, and I regarded them not, saith YeHoVaH. 10 For this is the covenant that I will make with the house of Israel after those days, saith YeHoVaH; *I will put my laws into their mind, and write them in their hearts: and I will be to them a God, and they shall be to me a people:* [72]

Here is a powerful difference that absolutely outshines the First Covenant. This covenant moves past external laws and brings them internally, writing them on the tablets of the heart! Inaugurating a covenant which affects the heart, God promised another amazing thing: "each person can know God!"

Hebrews 8:11

11 And they shall not teach every man his neighbour, and every man his brother, saying, Know YeHoVaH: for all shall know me, from the least to the greatest.

Believers in this covenant, in stark contrast to the former one, have close access to God. Believers can, therefore, know God first hand! That was not possible under the First Covenant, as those who approached God, within that system of the Law, had to be of one tribe, only. With the establishment of the New Covenant,

---

[72] Bolding and italics the author's

the Old, in accordance with scripture, decayed, became old and ready to vanish:

Hebrews 8:13

> 13 In that he saith, A new covenant, he hath made the first old. Now that which decayeth and waxeth old is ready to vanish away.

With this scripture, we recognize that a better covenant has arrived. Thus, we raise our sights higher to the place where Yeshua reigns forever: namely, at His Father's right hand:

Hebrews 8:1-2

> 1 Now of the things which we have spoken this is the sum: We have such an high priest, who is set on the right hand of the throne of the Majesty in the heavens; 2 A minister of the sanctuary, and of the true tabernacle, which YeHoVaH pitched, and not man.

This tabernacle in heaven, of which the one on earth was a copy, was pitched or erected by God. Heaven's Tabernacle is, in fact, the original!

Looking, back upon the tabernacle of earth, we see, once again, a shadow of the real one. As such, the High Priests which operated within the Mosaic tabernacle, were also a shadow of the High Priest of the greater tabernacle, the one in heaven. Looking then, at the High Priest upon the earth, we can understand more about the duties of the heavenly one.

On earth, the High Priest over the Mosaic tabernacle was ordained or appointed by God for the purposes of offering gifts and sacrifices. He served in that temple, and his duties, which were many and varied, were clearly specified by YeHoVaH. Thus, as the High Priest performed his duties, he became an example to demonstrate important aspects of the Heavenly Tabernacle and its High Priest, Yeshua.

RULERSHIP RESTORED

God restored many things to man, things that were lost at the fall. In this chapter, we see God restored "life", where death reigned. In accordance with the book of Ephesians, when one is born of the Spirit of God, they are seated in heavenly places in Yeshua. That place within the heavens restored something very important. Let's take a side step and look at that!

When Adam sinned, he lost access to the original dominion God gave to him and his wife. From the point of the fall onward, Adam and Eve were blocked by sin to that dominion. Thus, Adam and Eve became subjected to the fallen world. When Yeshua came He conquered sin and death. Yeshua, on behalf of all humankind, regained access to the original dominion God gave to Adam and Eve. That dominion is realized in the born-again believer's life, as God raises them to sit with Messiah in heavenly places.

Ephesians 2:4-7

> 4 But God, who is rich in mercy, for his great love wherewith he loved us, 5 Even when we were dead in sins, hath quickened us together with Messiah, (by grace ye are saved;) 6 And hath raised us up together, and made us sit together in heavenly places in Messiah Jesus: 7 That in the ages to come he might shew the exceeding riches of his grace in his kindness toward us through Messiah Jesus.

Verse 6 makes it very clear! Through our position in Messiah, we have access to the dominion Yeshua gained. From that place, seated in Him, we rule and reign so that in the ages to come, God shows the exceeding riches of His grace and kindness towards us.

Ephesians 2:8-10

> 8 For by grace are ye saved through faith; and that not of yourselves: it is the gift of God: 9 Not of works, lest any man should boast. 10 For we are his workmanship, created in Messiah Jesus unto good works,

which God hath before ordained that we should walk in them.

Of this place, we do not boast! It is nothing to do with our merit! God, through Yeshua, seated us in heavenly places. We are God's workmanship created in His Son, Yeshua, for the sole purpose of good works! Those works have been foreordained so we can walk in them! Part of those works is properly using our position in Messiah, to see the captives set free.

Just as Yeshua went about doing good works, so should we, as told in the book of Acts:

Acts 10:38

> 38 How God anointed Jesus of Nazareth with the Holy Ghost and with power: who went about doing good, and healing all that were oppressed of the devil; for God was with him.

Surely, this Tabernacle in heaven is far greater! Surely Messiah's priesthood is far greater, and thus, ours also.

A Far Greater High Priest — 10

Under every order of priesthood within the Bible, we see an altar and a sacrifice. Both Adamic and Aaronic order these. Adamic altars were made of stone. The altar within the Tabernacle of Moses was a brazen altar. Even under the order of Melchizedek, which is the priesthood order of Yeshua, there was an altar and a sacrifice. To see Yeshua's altar and sacrifice, we need to look at the book of Hebrews.

YESHUA'S ALTAR & SACRIFICE

Back in Chapter Six, we read something regarding the Body of Yeshua. Let's pick that scripture up one more time, and this time include a few more verses:

Hebrews 10:5-10

> 5 Wherefore when he cometh into the world, he saith, Sacrifice and offering thou wouldest not, but a body hast thou prepared me: 6 In burnt offerings and sacrifices for sin thou hast had no pleasure. 7 Then said I, Lo, I come (in the volume of the book it is written of me,) to do thy will, O God. 8 Above when he said, Sacrifice and offering and burnt offerings and offering for sin thou wouldest not, neither hadst pleasure therein; which are offered by the law; 9 Then said he, Lo, I come to do thy will, O God. He taketh away the first, that he may establish the second. 10 By the which will we are sanctified through the offering of the body of Jesus Messiah once for all.

Yeshua's body was offered as a sacrifice. As you read, that body was prepared by God for its special purpose: *to do the will of YeHoVaH*. In doing that will, Yeshua fulfilled the role of a suffering Messiah, that which the prophets prophesied throughout the Hebraic scriptures.

These First Covenant scriptures pointed to the sacrificial altar, and interesting enough, they also told of a normal practice of the priesthood:

Psalm 118:27

> 27 God [is] YeHoVaH, which hath shewed us light: bind the sacrifice with cords, [even] unto the horns of the altar.

Aaronic priests first bound their animal sacrifices to the horns of the altar, before the use of the knife to end the animal's life and spill its blood. Without those cords securing the animal to the horns of the altar, the animal, if it had the chance, would surely escape. Death was not welcomed!

Yeshua, on the other hand, willingly laid down His life for humankind. He followed the Father's will:

> Hebrews 12:2 b), in reference to Yeshua:
>
> > 2 who for the joy that was set before him endured the cross, despising the shame, and is set down at the right hand of the throne of God.

Yeshua's love formed the cords that bound Him to the cross as He laid down His life in fulfilment of YeHoVaH's will for our salvation. At that point in time, the cross became His sacrificial altar, whereby His blood flowed out to make atonement for the sins of the entire world. [73]

YESHUA'S HEAVENLY TABERNACLE

Yeshua, after the completion of man's salvation, entered Heaven itself, having made complete, with His own sinless blood, total atonement for sin[74]. His functioning priesthood far surpasses that of Aaron's order. Sacrifices in that order required continuous sacrifices. Yeshua's was once for all time, and with it God cleansed the Heavenly Tabernacle!

Hebrews 9:23-28

> 23 [It was] therefore necessary that the patterns of things in the heavens should be purified with these; but the heavenly things themselves with better sacrifices than these. 24 For Messiah is not entered into the holy places made with hands, which are the figures of the true; but into heaven itself, now to appear in the presence of God for us:

---

[73] According to some people, they believe the Ark of the Covenant was located directly below the crucifixion sight and Yeshua's blood fell directly upon the Mercy Seat.

[74] Hebrews 10:10 By the which will we are sanctified through the offering of the body of Jesus Messiah once for all.

> 25 Nor yet that he should offer himself often, as the high priest entereth into the holy place every year with blood of others; 26 **For then must he often have suffered since the foundation of the world: but now once in the end of the world hath he appeared to put away sin by the sacrifice of himself**[75]. 27 And as it is appointed unto men once to die, but after this the judgment: 28 So Messiah was once offered to bear the sins of many; and unto them that look for him shall he appear the second time without sin unto salvation.

Not only was the sacrifice once and for all, it also completely cleansed the heavens, in every capacity God saw as necessary. Additionally, it wholly cleansed all those who received God's plan for salvation.

> Hebrews 10:11-14
> 11 And every priest standeth daily ministering and offering oftentimes the same sacrifices, which can never take away sins: 12 But this man, after he had offered one sacrifice for sins for ever, sat down on the right hand of God; 13 From henceforth expecting till his enemies be made his

---

[75] Bold and italics added by the author.

footstool. 14 For by one offering he hath perfected for ever them that are sanctified.

Yeshua, also, has an earthly tabernacle, which is the believer. This aspect we'll cover when discussing the believer's priesthood.

LIFESPAN OF YESHUA'S PRIESTHOOD

People upon the earth have a limited lifespan and then they die. The same is true of those who entered any form of priesthood. At a certain point in their life, they died and at their death[76], their priesthood ceased. Yeshua's priesthood, however, has an eternal span of time, for He lives forever!

Revelation 1:17 b-18 Yeshua speaking says:

17 Fear not; I am the first and the last: 18 I am he that liveth, and was dead; and, behold, I am alive for evermore, Amen; and have the keys of hell and of death.

Attached to the priesthood of Yeshua, we see His priesthood is that of Melchizedek:

Hebrews 7:15-17
15 And it is yet far more evident: for that after the similitude of Melchisedec there

---

[76] Some ceased before their death.

ariseth another priest, 16 Who is made, not after the law of a carnal commandment, but after the power of an endless life. 17 For he testifieth, Thou art a priest for ever after the order of Melchisedec.

Yeshua's priesthood is forever, made after the power of an endless life!

YESHUA'S PRIESTHOOD SANCTIFIES

Under the Aaronic order, within the sacrificial system of the law, the high priest sprinkled the blood. In reading Hebrews again, we read:

Hebrews 9:11-13

> 11 But Messiah being come an high priest of good things to come, by a greater and more perfect tabernacle, not made with hands, that is to say, not of this building; 12 Neither by the blood of goats and calves, but by his own blood he entered in once into the holy place, having obtained eternal redemption for us. 13 For if the blood of bulls and of goats, and the ashes of an heifer sprinkling the unclean, sanctifieth to the purifying of the flesh: .

YESHUA'S PRIESTHOOD MEDIATES

A priest is a mediator, one who acts as a bridge between disagreeing parties. Mediators, within the Adamic system of worship, offered gifts to God, on behalf of man. They did what others could not do for themselves. Likewise, the Aaronic priesthood, did the same, however with the installation of the Aaronic (Levitical) the Adamic priesthood ceased! The only acceptable sacrifice under the Law was that offered by the chosen tribe of priests! With Yeshua, in the New Covenant which He inaugurated in His blood, the priesthood again changed. In fact, it was prophesised as such within the First Covenant.[77]

In Hebrews, we learn Yeshua's priesthood mediates:

Hebrews 9:14-15

> 14 How much more shall the blood of Messiah, who through the eternal Spirit offered himself without spot to God, purge your conscience from dead works to serve the living God? 15 And for this cause he is the mediator of the new testament, that by means of death, for the redemption of the transgressions that were under the first testament, they which are called might receive the promise of eternal inheritance.

Yeshua's blood, offered through the Eternal Spirit, purges the sinner's conscience. The

---

[77] Psalm 110:4

believer now shifts from dead works to serving a living God! It is for this reason, Yeshua is the mediator of this New Covenant. Through His sacrificial death, He redeemed the transgressors! He, the promised Saviour, the prophesied to Adam had come!

Genesis 3:15

> 15 And I will put enmity <0342> between thee and the woman, and between thy seed and her seed; it shall bruise thy head, and thou shalt bruise his heel.

In chapter One, we looked at this! There we saw that the Hebraic word picture of "enmity" showed *a powerful leader, with arms stretched out, whose deeds (work) touches people (nations) obtains victory by the breath of God.* Hebrews 9:14 calls that breath of God "the Eternal Spirit"!

This promised one, the Messiah was indeed an enemy of sin! Indeed, He brought division between the serpents seed and Himself, (the promised seed). He regained all Adam lost, and as the enemy of sin and victory over it, gave a great eternal inheritance.

Yeshua, as our High Priest, lives forever more as that mediator, our High Priest of a far better covenant. As such, He saves to the uttermost, meaning to the most extreme ends of all things in the lives of those who are willing to draw near and receive of His ministry:

Hebrews 7:25

> "Wherefore he is able also to save them to the uttermost that come unto God by him, seeing he ever liveth to make intercession for them."

YESHUA'S PRIESTHOOD INTERCEDES

We see from this last scripture that Yeshua ever lives to make intercession. In the book of Revelation, we see a wonderful picture of that intercession:

Revelation 8:3-5

> 3 And another angel came and stood at the altar, having a golden censer; and there was given unto him much incense, that he should offer it with the prayers of all saints upon the golden altar which was before the throne. 4 And the smoke of the incense, which came with the prayers of the saints, ascended up before God out of the angel's hand. 5 And the angel took the censer, and filled it with fire of the altar, and cast it into the earth: and there were voices, and thunderings, and lightnings, and an earthquake.

In looking at this passage, we discover that the prayers of the saints are seen in the heavens as "incense". These prayers are pictured as arising incense, offered upon the golden altar of incense before the throne. Next, we hear an angel (meaning, one sent to execute God's purposes) took the censer, filled it with fire from off the altar. Those added coals from the altar, is nothing else than the fire of the Holy Spirit. Next, the censer was cast to the earth. As a result, there were voices, thunderings, lightnings and an earthquake.

This scene is a beautiful picture of YeHoVaH answering the prayers to the saints, with the added intercession of the Mediator of Heaven, who lives to make intercession!

YESHUA'S QUALIFICATIONS

Yeshua, is qualified to be our High Priest by His perfect life, His perfect sacrifice, yes, by His precious blood which He shed for the remission of all sins! By this, He entered heaven itself, on behalf of all who'd believe. Through His love-filled blood sacrifice, He is heaven's High Priest of Whom, all can avail, *if only they believe in Him!*

- Yeshua's priesthood confirmed by God's oath, therefore, excels far above the Adamic priesthood, with its stone altar and animal sacrifices. It far surpasses in greatness the magnificence of the Aaronic order, with its Laws and ordinances, even though it foreshadowed Yeshua!

- Yeshua's priesthood, with its sinless blood sacrifice, cleanses the very conscience, removing all guilt! In this and other aspects, it stands operative within a much greater covenant.

- Yeshua's priesthood, falling within the order of Melchizedek, constitutes a greater order, whose service is forever, operative in Heaven's Tabernacle, and by God's mercy and power, affects believers upon the earth!

YESHUA'S SINLESS BLOOD

High priests, beginning from the Adamic order, offered animal sacrifices with blood. When it came to those animal sacrifices, YeHoVaH gave the reason for its offering:

Leviticus 17:11

11 For the life of the flesh is in the blood: and I have given it to you upon the altar to make an atonement for your souls: for it is the blood that maketh an atonement for the soul.

First, the life of the flesh is in the blood. That term, "flesh", here refers to animals, but in other portions of scripture, we know it also refers to human kind as well. Second, the blood was given upon the altar to make an atonement for sins for the soul, but only Yeshua's sinless blood can totally wash away sin! Third, we must remember something about the blood of human kind, which only God hears:

Genesis 4:10-11

> 10 And he said, What hast thou done? the voice of thy brother's blood crieth unto me from the ground. 11 And now art thou cursed from the earth, which hath opened her mouth to receive thy brother's blood from thy hand;

God heard the cry of Abel's blood as the earth opened its mouth and swallowed it. Yeshua's blood also, shed upon the earth, had a voice:

Hebrews 12:24

> 24 And to Jesus the mediator of the new covenant, and to the blood of sprinkling, that speaketh better things than that of Abel.

Yeshua's blood does not cry out with the same petition as that of Abel's blood. Abel's blood required a response of God to somehow pay back the violent act performed upon Abel as Cain cut off his life and priesthood, in its prime. Yeshua's blood, on the other hand, cries out for God's response to extend forgiveness and mercy, the punishment for crimes already paid! It speaks, therefore of better things than the blood of Abel.

As the animal's blood was sprinkled, under the Law, through the Aaronic priesthood, it was sprinkled in various places to sanctify:

- on the brazen altar (at its base)[78]
- on the horns of the altar of incense[79]
- on the priest's right ear, thumb and foot[80]
- on the people [81]
- on the Mercy Seat which sat on the Ark of the Covenant[82]

Yeshua's blood, that which speaks of mercy and forgiveness, once shed fell onto the earth, and was swallowed into the earth from the cross, and various other places such as the whipping post. Spiritually, however, Yeshua's blood was presented, after His resurrection, into the heavens to cleanse them. Just as the High Priest sprinkled blood upon the Mercy Seat in the Aaronic order, *(which typified or shadowed*

---

[78] Leviticus 4:7
[79] Leviticus 16:18
[80] Leviticus 8:24
[81] Exodus 24:8
[82] Leviticus 16:14

Heaven's Tabernacle) Yeshua's blood was sprinkled upon the Mercy Seat in heaven!

There seems so much more to write about the High Priesthood of Yeshua, as well as the blood of sprinkling, but as we close this chapter, at this point, please remember:

With God's action of choosing Yeshua, the High Priest's lineage changed from the firstborn nation, namely Israel, to the first born from the dead, namely Yeshua.

A Far Greater Priesthood in Messiah – Part 1   11

Here is the long-awaited chapter on the believer's priesthood, whose order has been identified in earlier chapters. Those earlier chapters, with its solid Biblical materials, formed a foundation upon which the latter chapter stands. From this chapter, onward, you'll see the believer's priesthood within the Melchizedek order unveiled. In doing so, please remember *the believer's changed life!*

2 Corinthians 5:17-21

> 17 Therefore if any man be in Messiah, he is a new creature: old things are passed away; behold, all things are become new.

18 And all things are of God, who hath reconciled us to himself by Jesus Messiah, and hath given to us the ministry of reconciliation; 19 To wit, that God was in Messiah, reconciling the world unto himself, not imputing their trespasses unto them; and hath committed unto us the word of reconciliation. 20 Now then we are ambassadors for Messiah, as though God did beseech you by us: we pray you in Messiah's stead, be ye reconciled to God. 21 For he hath made him to be sin for us, who knew no sin; that we might be made the righteousness of God in him.

In accordance with this scripture, a true believer in Messiah is a new creation. He or she, who is now in Messiah, becomes part of a new creation, *made through Messiah,* that creation of which never before existed upon the face of the earth. The essence of that creation is based on Yeshua's heavenly position, in which all believers partake. This will be discussed in greater detail, shortly. For now, let's take a personal look at a believer in Messiah.

Whatever sins happened in any believer's life, *prior to the new life in Messiah,* is no longer of importance *in God's eyes.* God wiped that record clean and seeing the vessel as pure and sanctified, deposits within the gift of the Holy

Spirit. This aspect of the believer's life is something that the first Adam knew, however, lost once he sinned. Life in the last Adam, Yeshua, moves to a much higher level than known by the first Adam:

1 Corinthians 15:45

> 45 And so it is written, The first man Adam was made a living soul; the last Adam was made a quickening spirit.

In the first Adam's action, death came upon all humankind. Through the last Adam, new life came. That new life is designed to take precedence over that former life. Through that believer's born-again experience, *the new birth*, he or she receives the gift of Yeshua's righteousness. He or she is made a minister of reconciliation to share the gospel with others, and is given a newly assigned role as an ambassador of the Kingdom representing God to others.

What God did through the last Adam is totally brand new. Believers alive *in the last Adam*, have something the first Adam never had ... *a position seated in the heavenlies.*[83] This is an important aspect to remember when thinking about the new birth in Messiah!

---

[83] Ephesians 1:3

Ephesians 2:4-7

> 4 But God, who is rich in mercy, for his great love wherewith he loved us, 5 Even when we were dead in sins, hath quickened us together with Messiah, (by grace ye are saved;) 6 And hath raised us up together, and made us sit together in heavenly places in Messiah Jesus: 7 That in the ages to come he might shew the exceeding riches of his grace in his kindness toward us through Messiah Jesus.

Believers, by the power of the Holy Spirit, are seated in the heavenlies with Yeshua. That position is important in living out the believer's life in victory, but it is also key when looking at the believer's priesthood. Let's look at Yeshua's position, **as High Priest**, in the heavenlies:

> Hebrews 8:1-2
>
> 1 Now of the things which we have spoken this is the sum: We have such an high priest, ***who is set on the right hand of the throne of the Majesty in the heavens***[84]; 2 A minister of the sanctuary, and of the true tabernacle, which YeHoVaH pitched, and not man.

---

[84] Bold and italics added by the author

Yeshua, as High Priest, sits at God's right hand! This is a place of honour, as well as a place of power. Scripture says God positioned Yeshua at His right Hand, after He purged our sins!

Then, Yeshua, as High Priest, sat down on the right hand of the Majesty on high[85]. "Sat down" denotes a place of rest. Yeshua as High Priest, sits. He rests in what atoning work has been done.

In addition, from this position, through His work upon YeHoVaH, God gave to Him all authority:

Matthew 28:18-20

18 And Jesus came and spake unto them, saying, All power <exousia>[86] is given unto me in heaven and in earth. 19 Go ye therefore, and teach all nations, baptizing them in the name of the Father, and of the Son, and of the Holy Ghost: 20 Teaching them to observe all things whatsoever I have commanded you: and, lo, I am with you alway, even unto the end of the world. Amen.

---

[85] Hebrews 1:3

[86] Greek word meaning authority, such as a judge uses. It is a legal, judicial, deciding ability by which a king rules.

Chapter 11 – Part 1   A Far Greater Priesthood in Messiah

Yeshua's priesthood, *that of Melchizedek,* **is a royal priesthood, that carries with it an undisputable & irremovable power of rulership.**

Conclusively, Yeshua's priesthood, operative from His heavenly position, operates, in part, through the completed and perfect sacrifice, which He gave on behalf of all humankind. This sacrifice, we must remember, neither time, nor circumstance, nor another person ever may count unworthy or worthless. Yeshua's sacrifice, in God's eyes, is totally acceptable and 100 percent complete.

Also, Yeshua's present High Priestly duties, such as cleansing the conscience of the believer, arises and operates through that same atoning work on the cross. In addition, His intercession, as believers draw near for it, stems from and arises through His victories on the earth, the culmination of which was on the cross. Every action done, at that time, was *not on His behalf,* but on behalf of all humankind.

Whatsoever work Yeshua does in His High Priestly ministry, He does from His place of rest, attained through that perfect atoning sacrifice.

From this, ministry all believers benefit!

THE BELIEVER'S POSITION & BENEFIT

By the power of the Holy Spirit, in accordance with the scripture in Ephesians 2, believers sit in Messiah in the heavenlies. That position, which is in Messiah, empowers believers to live out their lives in holiness, while giving them access to utilize Yeshua's authority. In addition, since this position in Messiah is clearly where the Holy Spirt placed believers, each believer must learn to also operate their life, *including the operation of their royal priesthood,* from that place in Messiah:

1 Peter 2:9

> 9 But ye are a chosen generation, a royal priesthood, an holy nation, a peculiar people; that ye should shew forth the praises of him who hath called you out of darkness into his marvellous light:

ROYAL PRIESTHOOD

It is this aspect of the priesthood that distinguishes the Melchizedek priesthood from others. Melchizedek was a King and Priest.

You hear that in His Hebrew Name, meaning King of Righteousness:[87]

Melchizedek	Strong's #4442
מלכי־צדק	Pronounced mal-kee-tseh'- dek
It is a word made from two words: 1) Melek which means King. 2) Tsedek which means righteousness. Together it means King of Righteousness.	

A believer's priesthood, as Peter declared, is a "royal priesthood". It carries with it an ability to rule, or to put it in simple terms, it comes with an ability to exercise the dominion Messiah received on behalf of all humankind.

DOMINION IN MESSIAH

In an earlier chapter, we highlighted Adam's commission,[88] where God gave him rulership or dominion over the earth. You read, at that time, Adam sinned and in doing so *lost access* to that dominion. It is imperative that we look at the fact that Yeshua regained access to that dominion. We see that in Yeshua's word to His

---

[87] Hebrews 7:2 To whom also Abraham gave a tenth part of all; first being by interpretation King of righteousness, and after that also King of Salem, which is, King of peace;

[88] First mentioned in Chapter One.

disciples, when He gave them, what we call the Great Commission, found in Matthew 28. While we looked at it just moments ago, let's look at it one more time, only slower:

Matthew 28:18
> 18 And Jesus came and spake unto them, saying, All power <exousia> is given unto me in heaven and in earth.

This "exousia", of which Yeshua holds "all of it", means that His authority, His ability to rule as a King is operative, in all situations. Due to that rulership, that authority, believers have a task to perform:

Matthew 28:19
> 19 Go ye therefore, and teach all nations, baptizing them in the name of the Father, and of the Son, and of the Holy Ghost:

As believers fulfil that commission, it is intricately linked with Yeshua's unlimited "exousia" or "ruling ability". Thus, they go and obey the latter part of that commission:

Matthew 28:20
> 20 Teaching them to observe all things whatsoever I have commanded you: and,

lo, I am with you alway, [even] unto the end of the world. Amen."

Unfortunately, while believers often recognize the regained *access* to the dominion given in Adam, many often fail to see its intricate connection in Yeshua, the last Adam. To put it in simple terms, every true born-again believer has access to Yeshua's victory which includes:

1. the first Adam's dominion, *restored* and
2. the last Adam's *irremovable authority*

We must recognize that since *the first commission was also fulfilled in Yeshua*, the two commissions: *one restored in Yeshua and one given after the cross*, work together to see the gospel go into all the world. Let's look at it!

MAN'S ORIGINAL COMMISSION

Earlier, we look at Adam and Eve's commission by God, before the fall. As we read it again, make note of the words "subdue" and "dominion", highlighted for your attention:

Genesis 1:26-28

26 And God said, Let us make man in our image, after our likeness: and let them have **dominion** over the fish of the sea, and over the fowl of the air, and over the cattle, and over all the earth, and over every creeping

thing that creepeth upon the earth. 27 *So God created man in his own image, in the image of God created he him; male and female created he them.* 28 And God blessed them, and God said unto them, Be fruitful, and multiply, and replenish the earth, and **subdue** it: and have **dominion** over the fish of the sea, and over the fowl of the air, and over every living thing that moveth upon the earth.

Earlier, in Chapter One, we defined subdue in the Hebrew, showing its meaning "to subjugate or bring under control". We showed the meaning of dominion as "to rule, to prevail over, to rule as a king".

For reasons which we are not told, Adam failed to subdue the adversary facing him, and equally failed to employ that delegated authority seen in his dominion in the garden. Instead, he willingly and knowingly disobeyed God. Once Adam disobeyed, he sinned and opened a door to death, which came upon all humankind.[89]

Once sin entered, the "image of God", with which God created in Adam, began to disappear in man, and rather quickly, too. Soon thereafter, Cain murders his brother Abel. That act of murder *is not in alignment with a person*

---

[89] Romans 5:12

operating in the image of God! However, we saw God's plan by which "enmity" would come between the adversary and humankind. God's plan of salvation, therefore, gave this sad beginning a better ending! Putting God's plan in the simplest of words, Adam's sin, with its penalty of condemnation and death, Yeshua removed at the cross, breaking sin's power.

Through Yeshua's obedience, life came to man instead of death. Through the free gift of Yeshua's righteousness, many were made righteous. That is the sum of the following scripture:

Romans 5:15-19

> 15 But not as the offence, so also is the free gift. For if through the offence of one many be dead, much more the grace of God, and the gift by grace, which is by one man, Jesus Messiah, hath abounded unto many. 16 And not as it was by one that sinned, so is the gift: for the judgment was by one to condemnation, but the free gift is of many offences unto justification. 17 For if by one man's offence death reigned by one; much more they which receive abundance of grace and of the gift of righteousness shall reign in life by one, Jesus Messiah.) 18 Therefore as by the offence of one judgment came upon all men to

condemnation; even so by the righteousness of one the free gift came upon all men unto justification of life. 19 For as by one man's disobedience many were made sinners, so by the obedience of one shall many be made righteous.

With this restoration by the son of God, the Holy Spirit dwelled within man, and thus, made it possible for man to once again, be restored to the image of God, expressing God's Divine Nature.

2 Peter 1:4

> 4 Whereby are given unto us exceeding great and precious promises: that by these ye might be partakers of the divine nature, having escaped the corruption that is in the world through lust.

With Yeshua's victory, the inaccessible dominion is now accessible! Thus, in Messiah, believers are fully equipped to bring things into their proper order, upon the earth.

THE GOSPEL COMMISSION

When believers in Messiah learn to fully function within their royal priesthood, exercising Yeshua's dominion, they learn to properly subdue, or bring things into alignment with God's will, through Yeshua's mighty name, authority and power. Also, they soon discover, that God gave believers much more than *a simple restoration from their fallen state.*

Believers in Messiah, unlike Adam, are seated in heavenly places in Messiah. From that position of authority, as believers live out their priesthood from that place of rest in the finished works of the cross, *the Kingdom of God readily moves into the lives of those who desire it.*

Speaking of the Kingdom of God coming upon the lives of others, Yeshua said:

Luke 11:20

> 20 But if I with the finger of God cast out devils, no doubt the kingdom of God is come upon you.

Therefore, to summarize Yeshua's words, when the Kingdom of God comes in an individual's life, the powers of darkness flee. Similarly, Yeshua said:

Mark 16:15-18

> 15 And he said unto them, Go ye into all the world, and preach the gospel to every creature. 16 He that believeth and is baptized shall be saved; but he that believeth not shall be damned. 17 And these signs shall follow them that believe; In my name shall they cast out devils; they shall speak with new tongues; 18 They shall take up serpents; and if they drink any

deadly thing, it shall not hurt them; they shall lay hands on the sick, and they shall recover.

Yeshua's commission, as Mark records it, when summarized, says that when believers go forth to preach the gospel, *(which is part of their priesthood responsibility)*, they cast out devils, they speak with new tongues, they take up serpents, aren't harmed by deadly things and as they lay hands on the sick, the sick recover. These activities show Luke 11:20's reference. As deliverance *is at hand, the Kingdom of God comes* upon those in need.

PUTTING THINGS INTO ORDER

Believers moving forward with the gospel, in the fashion of Mark 16, see God's kingdom come into the lives of others and at that same time, push back enemy forces, subduing them. Some people of whom believers may touch, will accept the freedom from sickness and disease as extended by the gospel, however, at times, others will soundly reject salvation. No matter the result, the Kingdom of God has come near them. This is what Matthew tells us:

Matthew 12:28

> 28 But if I cast out devils by the Spirit of God, then the kingdom of God is come unto you.

These activities of casting out devils, of bringing God's kingdom into the life of another, is *not walking like Adam*. If you remember, he failed to put things in the garden into subjection, or in other words, he failed to bring things into God's order.

These activities of the believer, as mentioned above, follow the lead of the Holy Spirit. Such individuals, therefore, do not walk like Adam who disobeyed God's commission. Such activities, rather, as Matthew 12:28 states, shows believers *walking like Yeshua*, responding like He did when He lived upon the earth.

With God's wisdom, through the power of the Holy Spirit, Yeshua succeeded in putting everything in order as God designed. Therefore, those operating in the believer's royal priesthood, sitting in Messiah in heavenly places, through the power of the Holy Spirit, bring everything upon this earth into Divine order.

In very simple terms, God privileged believers in Messiah to look forward to seeing the Kingdom of God come in and His will be done, first, in their own life and then in the lives of others, as they move out to preach the gospel. This is how the original commission of man, of which Yeshua regained access, coordinates and intricately connects with Yeshua's commission to go into all the world with the gospel. The first commission is now made possible and made greater, due to Yeshua's total, unalterable authority, and His Heavenly ministry.

Certainly, the original commission of man, once again accessible through Yeshua, and the great commission given by Messiah, go hand in hand, totally operative, *in and through the royal priesthood of Melchizedek!*

A Far Greater Priesthood in Messiah – Part 2

In looking at this former chapter with the powerful dominion and authority accessible to believers, it is wise to remember that the New Covenant priesthood of Melchizedek operates with more than its rulership aspect! It is a royal priesthood, indeed, but that "rulership" is best operative out of a relationship with God. Matthew records the words of Yeshua, where He spoke of the end of those who use His Name, yet have no relationship with Him:

Matthew 7:21-23

> 21 Not every one that saith unto me, Lord, Lord, shall enter into the kingdom of heaven; but he that doeth the will of my Father which is in heaven. 22 Many will say to me in that day, Lord, Lord, have we not prophesied in thy name? and in thy name have cast out devils? and in thy name done many wonderful works? 23 And then will I profess unto them, I never knew you: depart from me, ye that work iniquity.

In the original Greek language, the meaning of this verse is very clear. Many did cast out devils and did numerous wonderful works in Yeshua's name. After all, there is no name higher! There is no name greater! Yet, the ones doing these great works failed to develop a relationship with Yeshua. We know this because Yeshua said, *"I never knew you."*

This statement stands as a warning. Believers must ensure there is a relationship whereby Yeshua truly knows the individual believer, personally! It is of prime importance to establish that relationship, for out of it the kingly authority should naturally flow. It should spring forth because of the believer's intimate connection with YeHoVaH, *done for the benefit of the Kingdom of God, to bring Him glory.*

 **Such a close and inseparable connection begins with God at the *believer's altar*.**

ALTAR OF THE BELIEVER'S PRIESTHOOD

If Yeshua's altar, in every way, shape and form was unquestionably the cross, then what is the believer's altar? The answer is simple! It is the cross, also!

Matthew 16:24

> 24 Then said Jesus unto his disciples, If any man will come after me, let him deny himself, and *take up his cross*, and follow me.

Mark 8:34

> 34 And when he had called the people unto him with his disciples also, he said unto them, Whosoever will come after me, let him deny himself, and *take up his cross*, and follow me.

Mark 10:21

> 21 Then Jesus beholding him loved him, and said unto him, One thing thou lackest: go thy way, sell whatsoever thou hast, and give to the poor, and thou shalt have

treasure in heaven: and come, *take up the cross*, and follow me.[90]

In each of these 3 scriptures, Yeshua's message is the same: "take up your cross and follow Me". Therefore, we see, it is not enough to say we are followers of Yeshua! Surely, He walked upon the earth performing amazing signs and wonders, but His purpose was to "die" on a cross for the benefit of all humankind. Those who wish to be disciples of Yeshua have the same call, "to take up their cross!"

The apostle Paul used different words in his address to the Romans, however, he said the same thing, *and several times in other letters as well*:

Romans 12:1-2

> 1 I beseech you therefore, brethren, by the mercies of God, that ye present your bodies a living sacrifice, holy, acceptable unto God, which is your reasonable service. 2 And be not conformed to this world: but be ye transformed by the renewing of your mind, that ye may prove what is that good, and acceptable, and perfect, will of God.

Here, the picture is of a brazen altar of sacrifice, whereby the believer presents himself. He is

---

[90] Bolding and italics added by the author.

not a dead sacrifice, one that feels no pain, no struggles, no fire! He or she is a living sacrifice, not conforming to the world but rather renewing their thoughts. Then, the believer learns to prove out that good, acceptable, and perfect will of God.

As we learned earlier, the cords of love bound Yeshua to the sacrificial altar. So, too, do the cords of love for our Messiah keep dedicated believers upon this sacrificial altar. Such a living sacrifice is seen by God as holy, acceptable and considered our reasonable service. In other words, it is acceptable and expected.

> 1 Corinthians 15:31
> 31 I protest by your rejoicing which I have in Messiah Jesus our Lord, I die daily.

With every action in the life of Paul, the Apostle, he lived his life, not for himself, but for God. Paul put his service in simple terms, "I die daily." Later, in his book to the Galatians, Paul expands on his daily dying:

> Galatians 2:20
> 20 I am crucified with Messiah: nevertheless I live; yet not I, but Messiah liveth in me: and the life which I now live

in the flesh I live by the faith of the Son of God, who loved me, and gave himself for me.

Paul, an Apostle mightily used by God, saw himself as on the cross, dying more and more each and every day. The life that he lived on the outside was through the faith of the Son of God, Yeshua, Who gave His life for Paul. Paul saw his life, not as His own, but belonging to God:

1 Corinthians 6:19

19 What? know ye not that your body is the temple of the Holy Ghost which is in you, which ye have of God, and ye are not your own?

On those same lines, Paul crucified the affections and lusts that came by living within these clay vessels, our human bodies:

Galatians 5:24

24 And they that are Messiah's have crucified the flesh with the affections and lusts.

Galatians 6:14

14 But God forbid that I should glory, save in the cross of our Lord Jesus Messiah, by whom the world is crucified unto me, and I unto the world.

THE ALTAR ... THE CRUCIFIED LIFE

Believers, those who wish to live out their priesthood in Melchizedek, fully embrace the crucified life. Their priesthood, then, offers a life to YeHoVaH that is *separate from the world*, and fully accessible to the Spirit of God. No flesh rules over them! That separation and victory over the flesh happens as the priesthood begins, functions and ends *at the altar of the cross!* This lifestyle produces the ends of the priesthood that Peter, the Apostle described:

1 Peter 2:9

> 9 But ye are a chosen generation, a royal priesthood, an holy nation, a peculiar people; that ye should shew forth the praises of him who hath called you out of darkness into his marvellous light:

BELIEVER'S PRIESTHOOD & TABERNACLE

Earlier, you read that Yeshua has a heavenly temple! Here, you read that born-again believers are His earthly temple or tabernacle. We see that as we look at passages in the Apostolic scriptures, where reference is often made to the earthly body of believers as "the temple of the Holy Spirit":

Chapter 11 – Part 2   A Far Greater Priesthood in Messiah

1 Corinthians 3:16

> 16 Know ye not that *ye are the temple of God,* and that the Spirit of God dwelleth in you?

1 Corinthians 3:17

> 17 If any man defile the temple of God, him shall God destroy; for the temple of God is holy, *which temple ye are.*

2 Corinthians 6:16

> 16 And what agreement hath the temple of God with idols? for *ye are the temple of the living God;*[91] as God hath said, I will dwell in them, and walk in them; and I will be their God, and they shall be my people.

These three scriptures, a select choice of many, show that each believer makes up a unique part of the Temple of God. God dwells within each believer, too. As believers live out their lives, *their priesthood activities span every dimension of their life.*

As believers follow through in their commitment to serve YeHoVaH, they incorporate their priesthood, not as an outward order to which they belong, but rather as an integral part and expression of their new life in Messiah. Each believer is, therefore, mindful of

---

[91] Bold and italics added by author.

both the owner and occupant of their temple: namely the Living God.

In the closing section of this book, we'll look at expanding more on the lifestyle lived out by the believer, expressing day by day, the priesthood to which he or she is called.

THE LIFESPAN OF THE PRIESTHOOD

When looking at Messiah's lifespan in the order of Melchizedek, we see that is it forever, because Yeshua lives forever. New Covenant believers, while upon this earth, as we've shown repeatedly operate under the order of Melchizedek, however, one day, when the earthly life span of the believer comes to an end, that believer exits this world to live with YeHoVaH forever.

At that point, the dynamics of their priesthood on the earth ceases. From that point, onward, the scriptures say that, as priests of God and of Messiah, we reign 1000 years with Him:

Revelation 20:6

> 6 Blessed and holy is he that hath part in the first resurrection: on such the second death hath no power, but they shall be priests of God and of Messiah and shall reign with him a thousand years.

BELIEVER'S MEDIATORY EXPRESSIONS

Yeshua, as we have seen, mediates in heaven, acting like a bridge between heaven and earth. Those operative in the priesthood of Melchizedek, upon the earth, do likewise. This priesthood petitions God for mercy in the lives of others, those who cannot intercede for themselves.

1 Peter 2:5-10

> 5 Ye also, as lively stones, are built up a spiritual house, an holy priesthood, to offer up spiritual sacrifices, acceptable to God by Jesus Messiah. 6 Wherefore also it is contained in the scripture, Behold, I lay in Sion a chief corner stone, elect, precious: and he that believeth on him shall not be confounded. 7 Unto you therefore which believe he is precious: but unto them which be disobedient, the stone which the builders disallowed, the same is made the head of the corner, 8 And a stone of stumbling, and a rock of offence, even to them which stumble at the word, being disobedient: whereunto also they were appointed. 9 But ye are a chosen generation, a royal priesthood, an holy nation, a peculiar people; that ye should shew forth the praises of him who hath called you out of darkness into his

marvellous light: 10 Which in time past were not a people, but are now the people of God: which had not obtained mercy, but now have obtained mercy.

Living out our priesthood as believers, we must learn to recognize and understand the importance of following our Lord's example: taking up our cross to live the crucified life. As we offer "spiritual sacrifices" to YeHoVaH, perhaps the most challenging sacrifice we give is that of our free will laid down for His will.

This means we put every activity of our mind, soul, spirit and body upon the altar. In other words, we lay down our entire being in living the crucified life. That we place on the altar before Him! Even though costly, this is a very presentable and acceptable gift to God!.

In praying for others, let us remember those who have not yet seen Yeshua as Saviour. They, like each believer, require mercy. Prior to salvation, we as unbelievers lived in such a way as not to value Yeshua, nor the things of God's Kingdom. Perhaps it was because we knew not His Name, nor His amazing salvation. Nevertheless, until the day we accepted Him, we lived in darkness. This is good to remember, as we reflect on those who are now living outside the Kingdom of God.

Another acceptable gift to YeHoVaH is always petitions of mediation, whereby believers intercede for salvation of the lost. As we do that and are compelled out of love and obedience to follow the great commission, let us never forget that we were once recipients in need of God's Mercy. Having received it, let us desire the same for others.

USE OF THE BLOOD OF YESHUA

Many good books have been written on the topic of Yeshua's blood. Needless to say, we cannot cover much of this topic within the context of this book. Nevertheless, we can highlight a very important and direct connection with the precious blood of Yeshua:

Revelation 12: 11

> 11 And they overcame him by the blood of the Lamb, and by the word of their testimony; and they loved not their lives unto the death.

Indeed, let us be grateful for the precious blood which cleansed us and made us acceptable to YeHoVaH. Let us treat the blood of Yeshua with the greatest respect, never found guilty of treating it as a common thing!

Let us never forget the cost, by which we were purchased, nor the love that propelled our Yeshua to die in our place. Let us fully embrace that love, not only to receive, but also to release it, including in a mediatory capacity as we petition YeHoVaH of the harvest, also to send forth labourers into the harvest field!

Matthew 9:37-38

> 37 Then saith he unto his disciples, The harvest truly is plenteous, but the labourers are few; 38 Pray ye therefore YeHoVaH of the harvest, that he will send forth labourers into his harvest.

May that love, additionally, empower us, as priests of the Most High God, to thrust us forward to reach the lost.

Chapter 11 – Part 2   A Far Greater Priesthood in Messiah

קדושה ליהוה

Incense & Intercession — 12

Earlier, in Chapter 7 many things were shown regarding the change from Adamic to Aaronic priesthood. We looked at the rebellion of Korah, where he, two descendants of Reuben and 250 princes failed to recognize the changed order of priesthood. We also saw God's response to that rebellion, as well as His stamped approval on Aaron's priesthood. All New Covenant believers can learn to accept God's order of priesthood for their life.

INCENSE FROM THE PRIESTHOOD

This Melchizedek priesthood, the proper priesthood to which the New Covenant believer belongs and functions, rests its work in Messiah and His finished works. How delighted must

YeHoVaH be with it and subsequently, with believers who accept the shift from the operation of the Aaronic covenant to accept the royal priesthood of Melchizedek! Surely it must give a pleasing incense arising before the throne.

INCENSE FROM A LIFE ON THE ALTAR

As believers learn to avail themselves of their altar, *the cross*, surely a pleasing fragrance arises to heaven! As YeHoVaH sees this incense rising, He recognizes not only His Son's legacy working within His seed, but also the genuine priesthood of the New Covenant believer, which He ordained through His Son, for the benefit of all human kind. When, as believers, we present ourselves as living sacrifices before YeHoVaH, is it most acceptable and seen as reasonable service![92]

Surely, such a fragrance arising from the crucified life, pleases the One who paid such a high price for us. Perhaps that incense is so fragrant that it fills heaven as a certain fragrance once filled a room when oil was poured out upon Yeshua's feet:

---

[92] Romans 12:1

John 12:3

> 3 Then took Mary a pound of ointment of spikenard, very costly, and anointed the feet of Jesus, and wiped his feet with her hair: and the house was filled with the odour of the ointment.

INCENSE BY FIRE FROM THE ALTAR

Looking at the altar of incense, momentarily, that represents the copy in heaven, we note that the horns of that altar were sanctified with sacrificial blood. That blood made the altar set apart for God and at the same time, made atonement for errors, things that offended God. Believers need to learn and grow in their priesthood, and so, in this New Covenant era, they know the presence of the blood on the altar of incense ensures their prayers are purified.

Wrong motives, ambitions, selfish desires of the heart must die, but until they do, the prayers (the incense) rising upward, are purified by the blood of the Lamb! Of course, the Holy Spirit works with *His refining fire* to redirect the heart to respond more like that of Yeshua.

INCENSE ADDED BY YESHUA

Yeshua, in heaven, ever lives to make intercession.[93] His intercession, on behalf of

---

[93] Hebrews 7:25

those in Him, adds His incense to the life that lives in Him, while dying to self. Perhaps that is just another lesson learned by believers as they read this scripture from the book of Revelation:

Revelation 8:3-5

> 3 And another angel came and stood at the altar, having a golden censer; and there was given unto him much incense, that he should offer it with the prayers of all saints upon the golden altar which was before the throne. 4 And the smoke of the incense, which came with the prayers of the saints, ascended up before God out of the angel's hand. 5 And the angel took the censer, and filled it with fire of the altar, and cast it into the earth: and there were voices, and thunderings, and lightnings, and an earthquake.

INCENSE OF A HOLY LIFE

Many times, throughout the Word of God we read God's requirement that those who belong to Him must lead a holy life, separate and apart from the desires and ungodly behaviours of those who live solely to fulfil the wants of the flesh:

2 Corinthians 6:16-18

> 16 And what agreement hath the temple of God with idols? for ye are the temple of the living God; as God hath said, I will dwell in them, and walk in them; and I will be their God, and they shall be my people. 17 Wherefore come out from among them, and be ye separate, saith YeHoVaH, and touch not the unclean thing; and I will receive you, 18 And will be a Father unto you, and ye shall be my sons and daughters, saith YeHoVaH Almighty

A life, separated unto God, is called a holy life. In that separated life comes the aspiration of attaining goals laid out for us by Messiah. Arising from within are desires formed by the power of the Holy Spirit through a transformed life. Among the aspirations of such a life is an intense desire for souls for God's Kingdom, for His honour and glory. Once again, a life lived in such a manner, apart from the world and its lures, rising as beautiful incense to YeHoVaH!

MORE & MORE INCENSE

Surely, there are many more ways in which a believer's priesthood, as it is lived out before God, arises with a perfume of sweet incense, pleasant and delightful to YeHoVaH. For now, however, we'll close this chapter and this book with some incentives for you, the reader and hopefully born-again believer, to function in the priesthood of Melchizedek.

THE BELIEVER'S PRIESTHOOD

After walking through the various orders of priesthood in the scriptures, and recognizing the order of Melchizedek as our own, we know several things about our priesthood. It is:

1. **A HOLY PRIESTHOOD**

    Purchased with the precious blood of the Lamb, we are not our own! We are called to a life separated unto God, by which we live out our priesthood. We hold no other thing of greater treasure than our God and our service to Him. Walking away from the world and its lusts, we see those things with a temporal end as unworthy of our response, for the things of God are our enjoyment. We see true value lies in the lives of humankind, for whom we make intercession.

2. **A KINGLY PRIESTHOOD**

    As we are seated in Messiah, that position causes us to rest in what Yeshua has done. From that place of rest and position of authority, we fill the dual commissions to bring things into God's order, and to take the gospel to the ends of the earth.

3. **A GOVERNMENTAL PRIESTHOOD**

   This priesthood learns to govern all its affairs through its relationship to Yeshua, as it expresses the capacity of its royal rulership. At the same time, such a governmental priesthood is capable of interceding for all forms of governments on earth, no matter their status of righteousness. Earthly governments have grave responsibilities. Petitions for them prepare them to align with God's will to care for the people in their charge. Even unrighteous governments need prayer! Remember how Jacob blessed Pharaoh for the mercy showed to his son and family!

4. **A GOD-CENTERED PRIESTHOOD**

   As a priesthood initiated by God, the believer's entire life focuses on Him. In this focus and expression of our priesthood, we receive His sweet fellowship. Without that connection, how can true life flow! It is only through that fellowship with Him, and a willingness to die to self, that His Divine Nature comes forth. Thus, as we live out our priesthood, every aspect of it, including every word and deed, must aim at accurately representing God to others.

5. **A PETITIONING PRIESTHOOD**

    Petitioning God covers many things, amongst them, a sincere supplication to God for workers to go out into harvest fields! Certainly, part of this Melchizedek priesthood entails such requests. As we petition YeHoVaH, look for many harvesters and a rich harvest of souls for the Lamb of God is worthy to receive the rewards of His suffering!

6. **A SERVING PRIESTHOOD**

    This service expresses how we value God's Worth! As believers in Yeshua, we are called to touch both God and man. Our dying to self is worship, perhaps seen by God as of far greater value than verbal praises. We serve Him by doing and expressing His Will. That will includes touching the lives of others. Serving God also means to carry the torch of His Word, speaking it whenever and wherever possible.

7. **A BLESSING PRIESTHOOD**

    Priests bless both God and man. This order of priesthood first, blesses God by the way the life is lived: *obeying His Word!* Did not YeHoVaH say, *obedience is better than burnt offerings and sacrifices?*[94] Next, a priesthood blesses humankind, wherever and whenever possible.

8. **A MEDIATING PRIESTHOOD**

   Anyone, at any place and at any time, may have a need. The Melchizedek style of priesthood knows well the victory Yeshua gained and avails itself of its immediate access to the throne of Grace for help in time of need!

9. **A RESTORING PRIESTHOOD**

   There's power in the name of Yeshua, thus, the Melchizedek priesthood cries "Restore"! As a result, lives are pulled out of the hands of ha satan and set free to serve the Living God.

10. **A TEACHING PRIESTHOOD**

    Such a personal knowledge of YeHoVaH, as attainable by this priesthood, opens a door to share with others the ways of YeHoVaH. This is done by teaching the Word through example in lifestyle, which includes words and deeds.

There are probably more ways in which to describe the priesthood duties of a believer,

---

[94] 1 Samuel 15:22

including the cost in living a crucified life. This aspect of the priesthood operates through its altar, namely the cross. It is there we take our problems, our heart breaks, our goals and ambitions. It is there we let go of our desires and take up those of heaven. For the believer following the example of Yeshua, the cross will, in the end, glorify God!

THE BELIEVER'S ULTIMATE DESTINY

Here, before closing, consider a few more helpful thoughts, as you think about embracing (or further embracing) the Melchizedek priesthood. Remember, the kingly role is easily embraced, however, its true expression, which pleases God, arises from a life lived entirely for God. It is a life that fully embraces the cross! It is a life that uses the priesthood, with all its responsibilities, to further the kingdom of God.

Truly, truly, God's ultimate destiny for every believer is to look like, think like, move like, and be like Yeshua, in every aspect of their being. That aspect of a believer's destiny takes time, as the believer learns to die to self and yield to the Holy Spirit for development of God's Divine Nature within. Moment by moment, individual destinies unfold. These begin to take place as the believer learns to follow God's plan for them, a plan established at a much earlier time.

Ephesians 2:10

"10 For we are his workmanship, created in Messiah Jesus unto good works, which God hath before ordained that we should walk in them."

As the believer seeks the face of YeHoVaH, daily committing their life before God, living out their priesthood before His face, they learn to make good choices. Good choices, culminated into a few words, are decisions aligned with doing the will of YeHoVaH. Such choices propel the believer into actions, which obey the Word of God and His Commandments.

These born-again believers, men and women, hear and follow the Holy Spirit's leading, as He leads them into all truth. Those behaviours indicate the best results for a Christian's life and for a vessel operating in the Melchizedek priesthood.

Among those results, within the setting of the believer's priesthood, is a powerful *prayer and intercessory life*, which is perhaps better described as the development of a close, intimate relationship, *meaningful and precious* to both God and the believer. Relationships of that magnitude don't just spring up! These develop slowly, simmered over the burner of time.

Such a relationship makes the born-again believer a close, dear and trusted friend of God. Such a relationship cultivates, matures, and unfolds through every situation the believer and God walk through, together. Such a connection with God develops every moment of the day, as the seconds of the clock ticks by.

Relationships of this kind, in accordance with the Word of God, are not supposed to be rare! They are supposed to be the norm, where every moment of the day, the believer lives in union and fellowship with God.

The Apostle Paul, in his writings to believers in Thessalonica, put it this way:

1 Thessalonians 5:17

"17 Pray without ceasing."

Such a relationship with God burns with passion, ignited by the fires of the Holy Spirit, with the believer upon the altar of sacrifice. This all rests safely within the parameters of a covenant, in which God chose to dwell or tabernacle *within man*, to commune with Him.

Communion like this, manifested in a powerful priesthood, produces a oneness, where believers learn, day by day, to operate in a oneness with God, Who dwells in them. His love, His compassion, His mercy, His truth, and even the desires of His heart, when yielded to, flow from the believer's life to accomplish the acts of God, especially those operative within the believer's priesthood.

It was for all of this, including the special relationship possible with God, for which Yeshua died. His death and the atonement for sin makes it possible for a person to become a sanctified vessel, and hence a tabernacle, or place where God dwells. This relationship, however, happens solely within the parameter of the New Covenant. Only through that covenant, sealed in Yeshua's blood, can this relationship exist.

Such a covenant opens wide the possibilities for an intimate oneness with God, where two hearts commune as one. As you walk towards that direction, towards that oneness lived out, allow your relationship with God to be totally ignited by the Holy Spirit's fire. Live your life, dear one, fulfilling the priesthood, which embraces the following scripture:

Romans 12:1

> 1 I beseech you therefore, brethren, by the mercies of God, that ye present your bodies a living sacrifice, holy, acceptable unto God, [which is] your reasonable service."

Believers, like Yeshua, are the sacrifice, consumed by the Holy Spirit's fire. Such a life is a pleasing fragrance. Such a life is pure worship to God! In fact, like incense tossed upon a burning coal from off His altar, such a life is an

ARISING INCENSE

Which delights His heart!

APPENDIX

ORDER OF MELCHIZEDEK
(Messianic View)

As mentioned in the earlier part of this book, many Messianic teachers believe that from Adam to Aaron, the operative priesthood was Melech Tzedek (Melchizedek). Again, this information comes from extra-Biblical sources. According to their teaching, Adam taught this priesthood to his firstborn son, Cain. Cain abhorred his birthright, being the priesthood. When he killed his brother, he lost that priesthood, which later went to Seth.

The priesthood passed down the line to the firstborn son, but many firstborn sons, like Cain, despised their birthright, Esau for example. From Jacob, the priesthood was then split:

- Melech (King) aspect went to Judah ... the sceptre shall not depart from Judah[95]. (Reuben despised his birth right, sleeping with his father's wife).
- Tzekek (Righteousness) aspect went to Joseph ... the birthright belonged to Judah.[96]

---

[95] Genesis 49:10
[96] 1 Chronicles 5:12

YeHoVaH[97]

A Name to Honour

If, today, someone asked you to tell them the name of your earthly father, without hesitation you would declare it. If, for some reason, you did not know the identity of your earthly father, you would say so. You might even give an explanation as to why that might be so. Thus said, if asked to relate the name of your heavenly Father, today, would you do so with ease, or would you draw a blank?

Most of Christendom, today, is totally ignorant as to the name of the Father, as well as the way to pronounce it. As the author of this book, I would like to join the ranks of those who wish to relate that name to the world. When we stand before the Father on the day, we give an account

---

[97] *Based on information given by Michael Rood. Some from his work entitled, The Chronological Bible, and some from his YouTube videos. Look for Rood Awakening TV. For more information see page 28 of the Chronological Bible.*

for our deeds in this body, it would be a good thing to know Him, His Name and how it is pronounced!

Did you know that the name of the Father appears at least 6,828 times in the Hebrew scriptures? Scribes recorded it with four specific Hebrew letters. They are as follows:

י	Pronounced yode, or yod
ה	Pronounced as hey
ו	Pronounced as vav
ה	Pronounced as hey

For centuries, whenever the Jews come across these 4 letters they simply say, Adonai, or Ha Shem (meaning the name). They refuse to pronounce the name for several reasons, some of which we will look at momentarily. For now, let us look at whether their tradition affected Christianity. That we can easily do by looking at our Bibles to see the 4-letter name of the Father either written or substituted.

A quick look reveals that our KVJ Bibles, as well as many other versions, the 4-letter name presented to readers is a 4-letter English word, "LORD"[98]. Whether intentional or not,

---

[98] *In some translations it is GOD.*

Christendom has followed the ancient tradition of the Jews.

AN ANCIENT TRADITION

In early second century times[99] Rabbis hid the pronunciation of the holy name of God. They did this by omitting the vowel pointings, which are necessary to make the name pronounceable. Hence, as they carefully wrote the scriptures, their omittance of the vowel pointings made the name unpronounceable. Historians believe there were two reasons why they did this:

1. According to Josephus, Rome, under the rule of Domitian, 81 to 96 CE, put to death anyone using the name of the Jewish or Christian God.
2. Many believe that the Rabbis borrowed a tradition from pagans, whereby the name of their god was considered too holy to mention, so they called him "Ba-al" meaning Lord. The Jews adopted this practice and most still practice it today, even some Messianic Jews!

---

[99] Some scholars believe it dated even further back.

TRADITION CONTINUES

Bible translators followed their tradition for many reasons which are not presently known. It is possible, they forgot the pronunciation of the name, but more than likely, those who knew it, hid it.[100]. Whatever the reason, following this tradition caused Christians to continue in this tradition.

Does that tradition offend the Heavenly Father?

If indeed its origin was Baal worship, then we can give a resounding Amen to the fact it offends God.

In addition, as we look at scripture, we see the Almighty was not pleased with this, for His Heart desires all to enjoy salvation, including the Gentiles. How can that happen if they do not know upon what name they should call? Scripture [101] clearly says in the end times,

---

[100] *According to some, the Jews secretly knew the name.*

[101].*Ezekiel 39:7 "So will I make my holy name known in the midst of my people Israel; and I will not [let them] pollute my holy name any more: and the heathen (Gentiles) shall know that I [am] YeHoVaH, the Holy One in Israel.")*

Gentiles will know His name and call upon it to receive salvation. Obviously, for that to happen, they must know the name of YeHoVaH (יְהֹוָה).

AN HISTORIC DISCOVERY

Today, some Hebrew scholars[102] have searched the world over for Hebrew manuscripts. In doing so, they found many Hebrew documents which contain *the full name with vowels* and therefore, they know the pronunciation of the name. These scholars different slightly in that pronunciation[103], but nevertheless, they are making the name of YeHoVaH known today.

---

[102] Nehemiah Gordon, a Hebrew scholar, according to his testimony, found the name of the Father with all vowel pointings in the Aleppo Codex, and through his efforts and those of others discovered that name with vowels pointings in over 2000 manuscripts.

[103] In Canada we pronounce certain words differently than in certain places in the USA. For example, in Canada, we say "roof" pronounced "(rhoof) and some Americans say roof (ruff). Therefore, let us not worry too much about the exact pronunciation. Let us just learn to use it!

OUR SAVIOUR'S NAME

Our Saviour's name, as given by the angel was "Yehoshua", which means Salvation. *The name of the Father (יְהֹוָה) is hidden or contained in the name of the Son for Yehoshua contains, in the front, the* first three letters of YeHoVaH *(Yod, Heh, Vav).* See the two names in the chart below.

The shaded areas show the letters which are identical in both names.

Yehoshua[104]		YeHoVaH	
י	yode or yod	י	yode or yod
ה	hey	ה	hey
ו	vav	ו	vav
ש	shin	ה	hey
ע	ayin		

In looking at the Hebrew root of the name of the Father, pronounced *Yah-Ho **Vah'**,* and looking at another scripture, about the Promised One, we see a fulfilment of scripture from the book of Exodus:

---

[104] Yehoshua is shortened to Yeshua, like James is shortened to Jim.

Exodus 23:21
> *"Beware of him, and obey his voice, provoke him not; for he will not pardon your transgressions[105]: for my name [is] in him."*

In speaking of the Prophet, YeHoVaH said that His name would be in the name of the Prophet. the one to whom we all must listen and obey. This is one more proof that Yehoshua (Yeshua) is the fulfilment of the promise in that verse!

HONOUR THE FATHER'S NAME

It's time we honour the Father's name by speaking it out. We, at Cegullah Publishing, intend to proclaim and continually pronounce the name of the Father, as well as the name of Yeshua, for in this way, we believe we honour our God. While it breaks with the tradition of many, thus far, *as we have shared the news of the Father's name and use Yeshua's birth name,* reception among fellow Christians has been excellent.

NAME CHALLENGE

Now that you are no longer ignorant of your heavenly Father's name, we invite you to join the unofficial network of proclaimers of the

---

[105] *Please keep in mind that Yeshua bore the punishment for your sins. Your sins were not pardoned, but they were atoned!*

Father's name. We invite you to shout it from the house tops. In doing so, you bring honour to the Heavenly Father, our Saviour Yeshua, and the Holy Spirit.

Romans 10:12-15
"12 For there is no difference between the Jew and the Greek: for the same Lord over all is rich unto all that call upon him. 13 For whosoever shall call upon the name of YeHoVaH shall be saved. 14 How then shall they call on him in whom they have not believed? and how shall they believe in him of whom they have not heard? and how shall they hear without a preacher? 15 And how shall they preach, except they be sent? as it is written, How beautiful are the feet of them that preach the gospel of peace, and bring glad tidings of good things!"

Use the name of YeHoVaH and also Yeshua in your daily conversation with God and man! Join the others who chose to proclaim that name and watch YeHoVaH bless you for your obedience.

ABOUT THE KING JAMES VERSION

Scriptures quoted in this book *originate* from the KJV **public domain version** of the Bible, which means, no copyright exists on this version of the scripture. While some find this translation outdated, Jeanne, trained in the KJV still finds this version helpful, and uses it in all her books[106].

In using KJV, however, it is good to remember the following:

- Some words in the KJV have changed meaning over the centuries. To understand such words, look up the root word in its original language. In doing so, the meaning stands out. For example, KJV uses the word "conversation", however, in its original language it means moral character, or behaviour.
- When KJV spoke of humanity, they said, "man". When you read that word, or hear others speak about the scriptures using the term "man", know it refers to all humankind, not a specific gender.

---

[106] In later manuscripts, the author updated the more archaic words in the KJV such as wouldest or couldest.

Due to tradition, the name of the Father, YeHoVaH appears as LORD, or at times as Jehovah. However, in all Jeanne's manuscripts, YeHoVaH's name replaces the term LORD. To learn more read "A Name to Honour", located in the Appendix section.

SALVATION'S MESSAGE

Yeshua, when walking on earth, said this:
> John 3:14-18
>> 14 And as Moses lifted up the serpent in the wilderness, even so must the Son of man be lifted up: 15 That whosoever believes in him should not perish but have eternal life. 16 For God so loved the world, that he gave his only begotten Son, that whosoever believes in him should not perish, but have everlasting life. 17 For God sent not his Son into the world to condemn the world; but that the world through him might be saved. 18 He that believes on him is not condemned: but he that believes not is condemned already, because he hath not believed in the name of the only begotten Son of God.

During the time of Moses, the children of Israel in the wilderness, rebelled against God, at which time poisonous serpents infiltrated the camp, killing many of the people. After seeking YeHoVaH for a solution to the problem, Moses followed God's instructions and made a bronze serpent fashioned and erected it on a pole in sight of the people. Whosoever wanted to live, must acknowledge their rebellion against YeHoVaH, and in doing so, look upon the erected pole and bronze serpent, to YeHoVaH, who gave them life in place of death, then they would live.

Yeshua said, just as Moses erected that bronze serpent in the wilderness, He would be lifted for all to see. This referred to the event, in the future, of Yeshua's crucifixion. During the time when the serpent hung on that pole, whosoever wanted to live and not die from the serpent's bite must acknowledge their rebellion, their sin against YeHoVaH.

Likewise, for those who wish to live eternally, they must look upon the cross of the crucified One, to Yeshua, who provided life for them. This was an act of love for all humankind, necessary because man is born from Adam, and thus is born with an inherent sin.

Secondly, man sins. The consequence of sin is death, and eternal death, wherein man will spend an eternity in darkness, away from YeHoVaH. Unfortunately, there is nothing humanly possible to reverse those consequences. Even if a person had made a genuine decision never to sin again, and for some reason they succeeded, all their good deeds and good living would not erase the penalty of eternal death.

There is only *one way* for Eternal Life to touch a person's life. That way, Yeshua explained to His listeners, comes *through the cross.*

Salvation comes by understanding these facts:
1. Yeshua, being the Son of God and the fulfilment of the scriptures, never sinned.
2. YeHoVaH, on behalf of every human being on the earth, chose to make Yeshua become as sin, in His Eyes, so that Yeshua might pay the penalty for sin, for all of humanity.
3. Yeshua paid that penalty. He died on the cross and was buried in a tomb.
4. Three days later, He rose again, appearing to His disciples, to show them the reality of His resurrection, to show them God vindicated Him and made Him both Lord and Messiah.
5. Yeshua could not stay in the tomb, because "death" comes to all who sin, but since Yeshua never sinned, therefore, death could not hold Him in the grave.
6. All those who come to Yeshua, to receive Him as their Saviour, receive liberty from sin and from its horrible consequence, eternal death.
7. They enter YeHoVaH's Kingdom and receive eternal life, as well as another gift: **The Righteousness of Messiah.** After salvation, when YeHoVaH looks upon a

believer in Messiah, He sees Yeshua's perfect life and sees a redeemed believer, set aside for YeHoVaH. Since salvation has taken place in the believer, the Holy Spirit dwells within them.
8. All it takes to receive salvation from YeHoVaH is receiving His Messiah, fully repenting from sinning against God[107]. YeHoVaH even gives the believer the faith to receive His gift of Salvation!

The Apostle Paul put it this way:

Ephesians 2:8
"For by grace are ye saved through faith; and that not of yourselves: it is the gift of God"

When you pray the following prayer, realize we present it here to get you started in your walk with YeHoVaH. Living out your salvation depends upon your commitment to follow through *from this point, onward.* From the moment of your commitment and onward, dear one, please seek YeHoVaH for His help in all

---

[107] *And against man. When a person steals, etc. they sin against both God and man. PLEASE NOTE: all references to "man", either by scripture or the author, refers to all humankind, not a specific gender.*

things, including help to make your life align with truth, and in the end be a praise unto His name, forever!

SINNER'S PRAYER & LIFETIME COMMITMENT

Heavenly, Father:

I acknowledge before You, YeHoVaH, that I am a sinner. I understand sin's punishment is a life without You, for all eternity. Thank You for sending Yeshua to the earth, as the Messiah. I understand now that He died in my place, to take my punishment for my sins. I believe You raised Yeshua from the dead, and now that I accepted Him as my personal Saviour, my old life dies, and my new life begins.

I humbly ask You to forgive me of my sins, and as of this moment, I receive Yeshua as my Saviour. I open my heart to receive the works of the cross that You provided for me through Yeshua, and with Your help, I will walk away from my sin, turning my back upon my own will and ways. I will now live my life seeking to obey Your Word and Your will. Help me to live, from this point onward, in a manner pleasing to You.

One more thing:

Remember, this gospel message comes with power. When you hear it, the Kingdom of God draws near to you. When you repent of your sins and receive Salvation, the Kingdom of God moves within. You cannot see it, feel it, or tell it from an outward observance. It is accepted, received, and lived out by faith! Seek out other believers in Messiah and may God bless you richly as you live your life, now, completely for Him!

So now, be sure and tell someone! Remember that a person believes with the heart unto righteousness and confesses with their mouth unto salvation, as spoken about in *Romans 10:10*:

10 For with the heart man believes unto righteousness; and with the mouth confession is made unto salvation

SCRIPTURE INDEX

1

1 Chronicles 22:18 .. 19
1 Chronicles 5:12 .. 232
1 Corinthians 15:31 207
1 Corinthians 15:45 187
1 Corinthians 3:16 210
1 Corinthians 3:17 210
1 Corinthians 6:19 208
1 Peter 2:5 .... 60, 76
1 Peter 2:5-10 212
1 Peter 2:9 76, 191, 209
1 Samuel 15:22 225
1 Thessalonians 5:17 228
1 Timothy 2:1-4 113

2

2 Chronicles 28:10 .. 20
2 Corinthians 5:17-21 185
2 Corinthians 6:16 210
2 Corinthians 6:16-18 221
2 Peter 1:4 197
2 Samuel 8: 11 19

A

Acts 10:38 168
Acts 7:2 11

D

Daniel 11:32 b 255
Daniel 2:21-22. 91, 112

E

Ephesians 1: 187
Ephesians 2:10 227
Ephesians 2:4-7 .... 167, 188
Ephesians 2:8 246
Ephesians 2:8-10 ... 167
Exodus 1:1-6 80
Exodus 15:11-19 63
Exodus 15:13 65
Exodus 15:17 65
Exodus 19:1-6 66
Exodus 19:8 68
Exodus 20:24-26 71
Exodus 24:10-11 71
Exodus 24:4 70
Exodus 24:7 71
Exodus 24:8 182
Exodus 24:8 b 71
Exodus 25:9 72

Exodus 28:1 ..... 82, 135
Exodus 30:1-10 117
Exodus 30:34 119
Exodus 4:14-17 136
Exodus 40:33 b-35 151
Exodus 40:33-38 82
Exodus 40:34-35 74
Exodus 7:1 136
Ezekiel 14:14 40
Ezekiel 36:26 103
Ezekiel 39:7 236

G

Galatians 2:20 207
Galatians 3:8 52
Galatians 5:24 208
Galatians 6:14 208
Genesis 1:26-28 18, 194
Genesis 1:28 ...... 21, 22
Genesis 10:25 45
Genesis 10:32 46
Genesis 10:5 45
Genesis 10:9-10 45
Genesis 12:1-3 12
Genesis 12:7-8 48
Genesis 14:18-20 53
Genesis 18. 47
Genesis 2:15 21
Genesis 20:7 50
Genesis 3: 14 27
Genesis 3:15 ..... 23, 24, 177

Genesis 3:16-21 26
Genesis 3:20 30
Genesis 4:1 28
Genesis 4:10-11 181
Genesis 4:4 30
Genesis 5:24 34
Genesis 5:29 ...... 35, 42
Genesis 6:11-13 39
Genesis 6:3 37
Genesis 6:5-8 36
Genesis 8:20-21 40
Genesis 9:1 46
Genesis 9:13 42
Genesis 9:24-27 44
Genesis 9:8-17 42

H

Hebrews 1:3 189
Hebrews 10:10 172
Hebrews 10:11-14 102, 173
Hebrews 10:1-4 98
Hebrews 10:15-17. 102
Hebrews 10:18 103
Hebrews 10:19-20. 156
Hebrews 10:5-10... 170
Hebrews 10:5-7 100
Hebrews 10:8-10... 101
Hebrews 12:2 b 171
Hebrews 12:24 181
Hebrews 7: 5-7 54
Hebrews 7:11-14... 138

Hebrews 7:12-16 ... 142
Hebrews 7:1-3 55
Hebrews 7:14-19 58
Hebrews 7:15-17 ... 174
Hebrews 7:17 143
Hebrews 7:19 139, 163
Hebrews 7:2 192
Hebrews 7:25143, 178, 219
Hebrews 8:11 164
Hebrews 8:1-2 ...... 165, 188
Hebrews 8:13 165
Hebrews 8:3-5 150
Hebrews 8:4-6 152
Hebrews 8:5 124
Hebrews 8:6 145
Hebrews 8:7-10 163
Hebrews 8:7-8 162
Hebrews 9: 8-10 154
Hebrews 9:10 paraphrased 157
Hebrews 9:11-12 ... 159
Hebrews 9:11-13 ... 175
Hebrews 9:11-15 ... 141
Hebrews 9:13-14 ... 160
Hebrews 9:14-15 ... 176
Hebrews 9:1-5 153
Hebrews 9:23 158
Hebrews 9:23-28 .. 158, 172
Hebrews 9:6-7 154
Hebrews 9:8-11 140

I

Isaiah 5: 19-25 107
Isaiah 53:10 100
Isaiah 53:1-5 99

J

Jeremiah 31:33 103
John 1:14 104
John 12:3 219
John 3:14-18 243
John 8:32 14
Joshua 24:15 108
Joshua 24:2 11
Jude 1:14-16 34

L

Leviticus 16:14 182
Leviticus 16:18 182
Leviticus 17:11 180
Leviticus 4:7 182
Leviticus 8:24 182
Luke 11:20 198

M

Mark 10:21 205
Mark 16:15-18 198
Mark 8:34 205
Matthew 12:28 199
Matthew 16:23 92
Matthew 16:24 205
Matthew 27:51 155

Matthew 28:18 193
Matthew 28:18-20. 189
Matthew 28:19 193
Matthew 28:20 193
Matthew 7:21-23... 204
Matthew 9:37-38... 215

N

Numbers 16: 16-17. 88
Numbers 16: 28-30. 89
Numbers 16: 48-49 121
Numbers 16:10-11 .. 87
Numbers 16:1-3 85
Numbers 16:21 89
Numbers 16:22 89
Numbers 16:39-40 120
Numbers 16:41-49 120
Numbers 16:6-7 86
Numbers 16:8-9 86
Numbers Chapter 17 122

P

Psalm 103:19 112
Psalm 110:4 ..... 58, 176
Psalm 118:27 171
Psalm 145:17 114

Psalm 40:7 100
Psalm 89:14 114
Psalm 90:10 39

R

Revelation 1:17 b-18 174
Revelation 1:4-6 76
Revelation 1:5-6 144
Revelation 12: 11 .. 214
Revelation 20:6 211
Revelation 21:6 127
Revelation 22:12-15 110
Revelation 8:3-5... 178, 220
Romans 10:10: 248
Romans 10:12-15 ... 240
Romans 12:1 . 218, 229
Romans 12:1-2 206
Romans 5: 17-21 ... 109
Romans 5:12 195
Romans 5:15-19 196

Z

Zechariah 6:11-14. 137

BOOKS BY JEANNE METCALF

An Arsenal of Powerful Prayers [108]
    Scriptural Prayers to Move Mountains
Arising Incense
    A Believer's Priesthood
Above Artificial Intelligence
    Finding God in a World of A.I.
Bible Study Basics
    A Closer Look at God's Word
Candidate for A Miracle
    Wisdom from the Miracles of Yeshua
Foundations of Revival
    Biblical Evidence for Revival
His Reflection
    What God longs to see in His People
Heaven's Greater Government
    Behind the Scenes of Earth's Events
In The Name of Yehovah
    Biblical use of Banners
It's All About Heaven
    As Pictured in Scripture
Kingdom Keys for Kingdom Kids
    Walking in Kingdom Power
Molded for the Miraculous
    Why God made You
Our Secure Faith Heritage

---

[108] This is a book of written prayers of assorted topics to help believers live a stronger, active faith. No workbook.

Foundational Truths to an Unshakeable Walk with God

Releasing the Impossible
The Limitless Power of Intercession
Volume 1: Intercessions from the Author's Life
Volume 2: Intercessions from Biblical Characters
Workbook: Both Volumes compiled in Workbook.

Salvation Depicted in a Meal [109]
An Hebraic Christian Guide to Passover

The Jeremiah Generation
God's Response to Injustice

The Warrior Bride-
God's Kingdom Advancing through Spiritual Warfare

Thy Kingdom Come
Entering God's Rest in Prayer

Watching, Waiting, Warning
Obeying Yeshua's Command to Watch & Pray

When Nations Rumble
A Study of the Book of Amos

Worship in Spirit and In Truth [110]
The Tabernacle of David - Past, Present & Future

---

[109] Haggadah (Guide) for a Christian Passover. No Workbook.
[110] Good sister book to "In the Name of YeHoVaH We Set Up Our Banners".

ABOUT JEANNE METCALF

Jeanne believes the Word of God opens a door to help every believer to know their God. That knowledge, once gleaned and retained, makes strong believers to help them stand in the real world in which we live, no matter their vocation.

With these convictions in mind, Jeanne, inspired and led by the Holy Spirit, began to write in the 1990's. Soon she developed inductive[111] style Bible Studies and self-published them for her students to use. With her major goal to equip the saints, she found that her sound teachings, presented with clarity and simplicity, made an impact. As long as her listeners put in their valuable time to study scripture and took Jeanne's advice to call upon the Holy Spirit to help them, they became

---

[111] In the inductive Bible Study method, believers learn first by reading and studying the Word on their own, then they glean from the textbook. This study method often gives a better foundation to a believer's faith than sitting through lectures or speaker related teachings.

powerful believers, transformed, prepared and ready to stand in their generation.

Today, past students who studied the Bible with Jeanne, as well current new students, testify as to the validity of Jeanne's writing and teaching gift. They love the clarity and simplicity of the Word as she presents it in a refreshing straightforward format. Thus, they encouraged Jeanne to make her books more widely available.

Therefore, Jeanne began Cegullah Publishing, and then a year later, opened Cegullah Apologetic Academy. The academy, in addition to presenting accredited, Bible Study material, invites all believers to read or study the Word of God, and thereby, be strong in YeHoVaH and the strength of His might.

A greater availability of Jeanne's works (as well as other authors which Cegullah Publishing looks forward to publishing in the future), opens doors for more people to know their God and do exploits!

"But the people that know their God shall be strong and do exploits". Daniel 11:32 b

***

About CP & AA
CEGULLAH PUBLISHING & APOLOGETICS ACADEMY.

We publish books. Since their content is based upon the Bible, the Word of God, we consider our books treasures. Through these available treasures, we give opportunities for our reading audience to explore pertinent topics which steady, reaffirm, and help them to walk out their life in victory.

Our Vision
- To supply Christian, Bible-based materials to help readers study God's Word

  Our Focus
- To help our readers to know *what they believe and why.*

  Our Mission
- To provide bible studies, devotionals, teachings, and other educational tools to help readers to know their God and connect with Him.

  Our Publishing Motto:
- *Publishing the treasures of modern-day scribes.*

  Our Academy Motto:
- *Earnestly contend for the faith once given to the saints.*

CONTACT INFORMATION
www.cegullahpublishing.ca

www.ingramcontent.com/pod-product-compliance
Lightning Source LLC
Chambersburg PA
CBHW071112160426
43196CB00013B/2545